The Passion Paradox

ALSO BY BRAD STULBERG AND STEVE MAGNESS
Peak Performance

ALSO BY STEVE MAGNESS
The Science of Running

THE
PASSION
PARADOX

A GUIDE TO GOING ALL IN,
FINDING SUCCESS, AND DISCOVERING
THE BENEFITS OF AN UNBALANCED LIFE

BRAD STULBERG AND **STEVE MAGNESS**

RODALE.
NEW YORK

RODALE and the Plant colophon are registered trademarks
of Penguin Random House LLC.

Portions of this work were originally published in *New York*,
the *New York Times*, and *Outside*.

Library of Congress Cataloging-in-Publication Data is available
upon request.

ISBN 978-1-63565-343-4
Ebook ISBN 978-1-63565-344-1

PRINTED IN THE UNITED STATES OF AMERICA

Jacket design by Sarah Horgan

10 9 8 7 6 5 4 3 2 1

First Edition

To Caitlin. I love you.

And to Eric and Brooke.
Thank you for helping me when I needed it most.

To the coaches who ignited my passion:
Gerald Stewart, Michael Del Donno, and Bob Duckworth

Contents

Why a Book About Passion?

Our last book, *Peak Performance,* delved deeply into the art and science of human performance. We deconstructed powerful, evidence-based performance practices; described how the best athletes, artists, and thinkers apply them; and explained how you, the reader, could, too. Yet throughout our research and reporting, we couldn't help but realize that focusing on performance practices alone misses a crucial point. All the greats shared something else in common: An unrelenting drive. An eternal hunger. An inability to be satiated. Passion.

As part of our writing and coaching—of top athletes, executives, and entrepreneurs—we've been fortunate to develop relationships with many individuals who put tremendous passion into everything they do. They are people who, simply put, cannot be content. People who thrive on the razor's edge. Perpetual pushers of boundaries and limits. People who relish giving something their all.

And, without trying to sound brash, sometimes we notice this drive in ourselves. Perhaps you do, too. As authors, there are few things we love more than being immersed in the writing process. Our most trusted advisors warned us that starting this book before finishing our last was a bad idea, but we couldn't help ourselves. Even though we had some doubts (e.g., "It's too soon for our next book . . ."), the blank page sucked us in, and there was nothing we could do to resist its pull. We just *had* to pursue our ideas and put pen to paper.

And though we're glad we chose to write this book when we did, we'd be remiss not to acknowledge that this urge to keep pushing and pushing also has a dark side, one that extends beyond just reasonable doubts. Passion often comes at the expense of time and energy spent on family, friends, and other activities, including the simple joys of life. Too much passion, especially without equally strong self-awareness (a topic we'll explore later on), can completely uproot your life and lead to burnout. This realization, or dilemma, really, is shared by just about every passionate person whom we've come to know. There's no way around it; when you are deep in the throes of a passion, when you're really going for something, it can seem as if nothing else matters. This can be a good thing, a bad thing, or, more often than not, a bit of both at the same time.

Observing this passionate drive firsthand in Olympic athletes, groundbreaking inventors, original artists, and successful entrepreneurs, as well as experiencing it in ourselves, led us to wonder: *From where does this intense feeling of passion come? How can one find it and what fuels it? How should one make the decision to pursue a passion that appears to conflict with other obligations? What makes passion disappear? Is it always positive? Or is it not so different from an addiction? Is there a* right *way to live with passion? To go "all-in" on something?*

. . .

COMMON ADVICE IS TO FIND AND FOLLOW YOUR PAS-
sion; to *be* passionate. It's what parents, teachers, coaches, and
commencement speakers champion. And yet, at the same time,
there's a growing cultural chorus that says following your passion is an irresponsible, if not reckless, endeavor: a path to *dis-
satisfaction*, poor health, and unease. The truth is that there's
merit in both arguments. As you'll see in the coming pages, as
much as our culture likes to simplify things—to make them
black or white, this or that—passion isn't so straightforward.
Yes, passion can be a blessing; it's a hallmark of mastery and a
precursor to great success. But if it's not pursued thoughtfully
and handled carefully, passion can quickly become a curse,
something that is far more destructive than it is productive.
This dark kind of passion is especially prevalent in a culture
that conditions us to crave quick fixes and instant gratification,
tempts us to judge ourselves by the number of "followers" or
"friends" we have on social media, and repeatedly tells us that
"winning isn't everything, it's the only thing"; a culture that is
achievement-oriented and compels us to focus solely on results
at all costs.

Fortunately, as we'll show you in the coming pages, the
choice to pursue passion—and equally as important, whether
it goes in a positive or negative direction—is largely up to you.
Passion, when approached in the right way, is an ongoing practice. A practice that leads to not only a wonderful experience of
working, but also a wonderful experience of living.

THIS BOOK BEGAN AS AN INTIMATE EXPLORATION TO
better understand how we, Brad and Steve, could live with

passion in a constructive, healthy, and sustainable way.* We scoured the literature, reading texts from biology, psychology, anthropology, and philosophy; interviewed cutting-edge researchers from across disciplines and all over the world; met with and studied not only individuals whose passion built them up, but also those whose passion broke them down; and looked deep inside ourselves, discovering the good, the bad, and the ugly about our own respective relationships with passion.

Perhaps you have an idea of where you fall on the passion spectrum. Maybe you have an inkling of a career path or business idea you want to pursue, but you have doubts or fears. Or perhaps you're contemplating going all-in on an idea, whether that means starting a company or training to become an elite athlete. Maybe you're already following your passion but you're feeling the beginning of burnout, or you're neglecting other aspects of your life, such as your friends, family, or just experiencing joy outside your chosen pursuit. Or maybe you're feeling all out of a passion that once fueled you. No matter where you are in the passion process, this book will help get you on track. You'll learn how to manage your relationship with passion and cultivate the kind of passion that lights you up rather than burns you out or sets your life on fire.

---

* The initial step in what eventually became this book was an article Brad wrote for *Outside* magazine titled "What Underlies the Relentless Pursuit of Excellence." Certain sections of that article appear virtually unaltered in the following pages, as does some of Brad's writing from *New York* magazine and the *New York Times*. Brad thanks these publications for allowing him to first explore some of the ideas detailed in this book.

1

Passion Must Be Handled with Care

"Nothing is as important as passion. No matter what you want to do with your life, be passionate. The world doesn't need any more gray. On the other hand, we can't get enough color. Mediocrity is nobody's goal, and perfection shouldn't be either. We'll never be perfect. But remember these three P's: Passion plus persistence equals possibility."

—Jon Bon Jovi, 2001 commencement address, Monmouth University, West Long Branch, New Jersey[1]

Odds are, the passion described by Bon Jovi—the wholehearted pursuit of an activity with enthusiasm, fire, and zeal—is the kind with which you're familiar. It's celebrated widely and encouraged in nearly all settings, from the classroom to the workplace to the playing field. If you could just discover your passion and pursue it, the story goes, everything else will fall into place. But in reality, it doesn't always work like that. Even if you find a passion to pursue, you're probably not given much, if any, guidance on what happens next. While there are plenty of voices telling you to *find* your passion, there are hardly any telling you *how to be* passionate.

The seemingly straight line to success, happiness, and ful-fillment that passion promises is almost always a more compli-cated route littered with potential wrong turns. In the words of Elon Musk, Silicon Valley mogul and founder of Tesla and SpaceX, "The reality is great highs, terrible lows, and unrelent-ing stress."[2] Consider just a few of the negative paths that pas-sion can lead you down:

- **You become a slave to external results and validation.** Following early success, the desire for more—more money, more fame, more followers—can easily take over. Your initial passion for *doing* an activity turns into a passion for achievement and results. You tie your self-worth to external validation, and the experience of a failure, or even just a plateau of mod-erate success, becomes devastating, rattling you to the core. Your enjoyment decreases (at best) and you become anx-ious, depressed, and unethical (at worst).

- **You become blind to everything but your passion.** You throw yourself so fully into a pursuit that you neglect everything outside it. Your marriage falls apart. Your children grow up without you realizing it. You ignore your health. You may feel good in the moment—after all, you are consumed by something you love—but years pass and you look back with regret on how you spent your time.

- **You burn out.** Surrendering completely to passion may work for a day, a month, or even a year. But if left unchecked, most passions burn bright and burn short. It's not that you don't want to pace yourself, but simply that you can't. You're far too overwhelmed by the acute pull of passion to realize the emotional and physical effort you are putting forth may be unsustainable. Before you know it, you run out of energy. What could have been a lifetime of passion and meaningful work instead looks more like a short bout of reckless excitement.

- **You lose joy.** There is also a risk that your passion's spark will dim slowly over time. A familiar story goes like this: You turn what started off as a wonderful hobby into a job (*Blessed!*); then you realize that what once was a wonderful hobby soon starts to feel like a job (*This isn't what I thought it would be like*); and it's not long before you start to question how something you once loved can seem like a chore (*How on earth did this happen?*). Though you never thought such a turn was possible, you come to dread your passion.

volleyball

There is, of course, a different—and far better—kind of passion. It emerges when you become wrapped up in an activity primarily for the joy of doing the activity itself. When you experience success with humility and failure with temperate resolve. When your goal becomes your path and your path becomes your goal. When your passion is fueled by deep purpose and is in harmony with the rest of your life. When you practice mindful self-awareness to pierce through the tidal inertia that passion can create, giving you control over your passion so your passion doesn't control you. When you feel alive not just for a few months or years but for an entire career or lifetime. *This* is the passion we all crave. *This* is the best kind of passion.

Almost all passions begin as enthusiastic pursuits. No one wants to burn out, throw their lives out of balance, or lose joy. Passion's positive and negative paths—the good and bad kind of passion—arise from the same place; it's just that if you don't proactively prevent passion from veering off course, it's likely to do so, oftentimes without you even realizing it. Put differently, passion is fragile, and it must be handled with care. This is why research shows that passion isn't just linked to happiness, health, performance, and life satisfaction, but also to anxiety, depression, burnout, and unethical behavior.

Though lots has been written on how to find your passion, much of it is misguided, rife with clichés while short on evidence. And, as you're starting to see, finding your passion is only half the battle anyway. Knowing how to sustain and channel it in a productive and healthy manner is the other— and equally important—half. Unfortunately, that half is rarely, if ever, discussed. As a result, far too often passion goes awry and people suffer from some version of the negative repercussions described above.

Passion is fragile, and it must be handled with care.

This book aims to change that. To show you how you can find and cultivate passion and how you can manage its immense power for good. We'll show you that what direction your passion takes is a choice, not a predetermined destiny. We'll give you practical tools to ensure that your passion burns bright, long, and in harmony with the rest of your life. And we'll do this without using trite clichés that dominate so many other books about this topic. We'll be authentic and honest, bringing to bear not only the latest scientific evidence but also the thinking of some of the world's most considerate poets and philosophers.

In order to achieve this goal, we'll undergo a thorough exploration of passion. We'll examine both the biological and psychological drivers that give rise to passion, as well as the stories of extraordinarily passionate individuals. Some of these stories will be positive, like those of Olympic swimming star Katie Ledecky and investor Warren Buffett; others will be cautionary tales, like those of the fraudulent businessman Jeffrey Skilling of Enron and baseball cheat Barry Bonds. We'll question the merits of living a "balanced" life, explore how self-awareness prevents future regret, and discuss the importance of the stories we tell ourselves about ourselves. We'll learn that passion is not an emotion that should be left to its own devices but rather one that should be harnessed with deliberate intention. But before we do any of that, in order to lay the groundwork for how we can live with the best kind of passion, we must first gain an understanding of its roots. We'll start by traveling back in time to a distant yesterday, when the notion of passion first emerged.

PASSION PRACTICES

- Everyone tells us to find our passion but no one tells us how to find it, let alone how to live with it.
- While most passions start off as positive endeavors, they often take turns for the worse.
- If you don't proactively manage your passion, you put yourself at risk for:
  - Becoming a slave to external validation and results.
  - Burnout.
  - Regret.
  - Loss of joy.
- If you do proactively manage your passion, however, living with passion leads to improved health, happiness, and overall life-satisfaction.
- In other words, there is both good passion and bad passion. And what direction your passion takes is largely up to you.

2

The Origins of Passion
A Brief History of Suffering and Love

Born out of the Latin word *passio*, which means "suffering," for the vast majority of history, passion meant just that: suffering, misery, and anger. Initially, the suffering that passion alluded to was narrow, used to describe a particular person and a particular instance of anguish: the unremitting torture that Jesus Christ faced during his crucifixion. "The word was singularly related to Christ," explains professor Timothy K. Beal, chair of the Department of Religious Studies at Case Western Reserve University, "and it was completely tied up in his suffering."[1] Some viewed Christ's death as tragic, whereas others believed there was a profound purpose behind it. Either way, for nearly a thousand years, *passio* was dedicated exclusively to describing the suffering of Christ. To wish *passio* upon anyone, or to instruct anyone to pursue it, would have been viewed not as supportive or inspirational but as toxic and harmful.

Over time, however, the definition of *passio* broadened. By the eleventh century, *passio* had expanded outside of religion, its usage now referring to all suffering and pain—both physical and psychological—and in all people. Although still far different from the way passion is used today, its definition was no longer tied to Christ. A few hundred years later, as Europe emerged from the Dark Ages, so, too, did passion emerge from its dark meanings. It wasn't long before the European Renaissance brought about a literal transformation of the word from *passio* to *passioun* to *passion*. With each turn, the word assimilated new meanings, transitioning from suffering to rage to love and, finally, to overwhelming desire. The creative arts are at least partially to thank for the transformation. This began with Geoffrey Chaucer, who, in his epic collection of stories, *The Canterbury Tales*, deployed passion to denote not suffering but rather a more generalized uncontrolled emotion. Other authors followed, employing passion in what at the time were novel ways. In 1588, Shakespeare used passion to describe not a negative emotion but a highly sought-after one. In the drama *Titus Andronicus*, Shakespeare co-opted the word to signify romantic lust and desire, writing, "And that my sword upon thee shall approve, / And plead my *passions* for Lavina's love."[2] With Shakespeare's prose, passion was shedding its roots in suffering and shifting toward a more attractive, positive meaning.

Still, it wasn't until the eighteenth century that passion became broadly associated with a more widespread zeal: a love and desire not just for another person, but also for some sort of pursuit or activity. And even then, the word's rise to ubiquity has been a slow one. Phrases like "follow your passion" or "find your passion" didn't enter the common vernacular until the mid-1970s. However, at that point, passion quickly became all the

In many ways, passion and suffering are still very much connected.

rage, and it's stayed that way ever since. In the '70s, the baby boomers were coming of age and embracing a can-do, "you get out what you put in" attitude. World War II seemed long in the past and the Vietnam War was coming to an end. The Western ideal began to shift from security to self-actualization, a trend that only accelerated with Generation X and now Millennials. By the time Bon Jovi gave his commencement speech to Monmouth University students in 2001, positive and inspirational phrases including the word *passion* were blossoming and becoming ever more popular. Today, one would think that passion is key to living a good and productive life. We're told we must do whatever it takes to find and follow our passion and that our careers, relationships, and hobbies are all better if they're fueled by it. But as you'll soon see, we shouldn't be so quick to write off the word's original meaning. Because in many ways, passion and suffering are still very much connected.

A CHEMICAL REACTION: THE BIOLOGY OF PASSION

The sensation of being wholly consumed by an activity, idea, or person is familiar to anyone who has had even just a brief dance with passion. Whether you become passionate about someone or something, the reaction is much the same. Your world narrows and the only thing that seems to matter is the object or activity of desire. Your romantic crush becomes all you can think about. You can't step away from the canvas. Even though your body is at dinner with your family, your mind is elsewhere, fixated on the new product you're launching or how you could rewrite the second sentence in the fifth paragraph on the thirty-fourth page of your book. Complete tunnel vision. Full-on immersion. Passion's got ahold of you.

This overwhelming feeling of attachment is birthed deep in our brain, where it's fueled by a powerful neurochemical called dopamine. Dopamine excites and arouses us, focusing our attention on whatever it is we are working toward. Under its influence, we feel revved up and alive. As dopamine courses through our brain, making its way from the primitive areas to more recently evolved ones, it sets off a cascade of neural reactions that push us toward a goal and create an expectation that a reward will soon follow: *If I only finish this book, I'll feel better. When I finally launch this new product, I'll be satisfied. If I can just be with that woman, I'll be happy. Once my work is on display at the gallery, I'll find some peace.*

And yet when you're under passion's spell, the reward you think you're chasing—usually some sort of contentment or satiation—is merely an illusion. If you accomplish your goal on Monday, perhaps you feel content for a moment, but odds are, you'll be hungry again by Tuesday.

There's a biological basis for this ceaseless yearning. Unlike other feel-good neurochemicals that are released *after* you've accomplished a goal, the far more potent dopamine is released *prior*, during the pursuit. This timing had an important evolutionary purpose. Our hunter-gatherer ancestors could not afford to be content upon meeting their immediate nutritional demands. They needed to continue accumulating food in order to prepare for inevitable times of scarcity. As a result, our species evolved so that dopamine—the striving neurochemical—gives rise to feelings of intense desire and often overpowers other neurochemicals that make

> When you're under passion's spell, the reward you think you're chasing—usually some sort of contentment or satiation—is merely an illusion. We don't get hooked on the feeling associated with achievement, we get hooked on the feeling associated with the chase.

We're not wired to simply be content. We're wired to keep pushing.

us feel content and satisfied. We don't get hooked on the feeling associated with achievement, we get hooked on the feeling associated with the chase. Dopamine is the molecule of desire and motivation. This simple yet powerful biological truth is responsible for some of history's greatest achievements, from the survival of the human species yesterday to groundbreaking scientific discoveries today. In short: We're not wired to simply be content. We're wired to keep pushing.

WHEN THE LEGENDARY ULTRARUNNER ANN TRASON was just two years old, her parents tied bells to her shoes. "I was always running around and they needed a way to track me," she recalls. Although her childhood predated the recent surge in diagnosing children with attention-deficit hyperactivity disorder (ADHD), Trason, now fifty-nine, says she would have been a fine candidate for the diagnosis. Emerging science suggests that individuals with ADHD tendencies might be less sensitive to dopamine, meaning they need even more of the neurochemical to feel content.[3] This is liable to predispose them to pursuing activities with relentless fervor, since doing so releases dopamine. For Trason, who remembers struggling to sit still and pay attention in school, running became an outlet, a place she could expend all her bottled-up energy and express her endless drive.

Shortly after high school, Trason discovered ultrarunning, a sport that involves races lasting upward of twenty hours and that makes running a marathon look like child's play. Pounding out 120-mile training weeks and running in 100-mile races gave her an otherwise hard-to-find sense of fulfillment. But it was always fleeting. She could have been satisfied many times during her running career, like when she won the American River 50 Mile Endurance Run in 1985 or the 100-mile-long Western States Endurance Run in 1989, or when she set both the Western States and Leadville Trail 100 course records in 1994 (all significant races that many ultrarunners compete in only once, let alone win). But Trason kept coming back for more. "I always had this urge to see what else I could do," she says. It was an urge that propelled her to become the most decorated ultrarunner of all time and to break down gender barriers that transcended running to affect all endurance sports. During her career, Trason broke over twenty world records, won the Western States— the most prestigious ultramarathon—*fourteen times,* and set countless course records, many of which still stand today.

We asked Trason—who, in addition to her running prowess, is highly educated and very reflective—about her innate hardwiring, about the little girl whose parents tied bells to her shoes. She had this to say: "I often wonder about dopamine. I always had this yearning to push, push, push—to see what I was made of, to beat myself and then keep going for more. It never went away. Biochemistry isn't everything, but I have to imagine it's a factor."[4]

The latest scientific research supports Trason's hunch. Some studies show that up to 40 percent of our personality may be inherited. Professor C. Robert Cloninger, a psychiatrist at Washington University's School of Medicine in St. Louis, Missouri, recently developed a system for evaluating the heritable part of personality, referred to as *temperament.* His research suggests that there is a link between our inborn temperaments and our sensitivity to specific neurochemicals.[5] In particular, he found that "persistence," one of his four major temperament styles, is closely associated with an insensitivity to dopamine. Remember, dopamine is released during the pursuit of goals, so it's not surprising that people who are insensitive to it (and thus need more of it to feel good) embody persistence, demonstrating unwavering determination and relentless drive. The more dopamine someone needs to feel good, the more willing she is to strive for and chase after ridiculously challenging rewards, even if doing so turns out to be detrimental to her in some way. In other words, she's got to get her dopamine fix. Although we like to think that personality traits like persistence result from hard work or how we were raised, that's far from the whole story. Some of us, like Trason, are born with a predisposition to passion. Yet it's also true that the biology of passion can come to affect us all.

The more someone repeats an activity—especially ones that yield positive feedback, be it winning gold medals, achieving promotions, or luring in romantic partners—the more they crave dopamine. Each time we pursue such endeavors, dopamine is released, increasing our arousal, attention, and motivation. Over time, and in a process similar to other addictive substances, our brains become less sensitive to dopamine, meaning we need more of it to feel good. This craving, if you will, leads us back to the pursuit, which triggers the release of yet more dopamine. And so a cycle of longing, and one that is inherently resistant to contentment, persists. It's worth reiterating that this cycle is a natural one. It results from our evolutionary programming, which pushes us to become addicted to the pursuit of rewards, not the achievement of them.

In his book *The Biology of Desire*, neuroscientist Marc Lewis writes that changes in dopamine requirements, meaning you need more of it to feel good, are caused by the "repetition of . . . powerful experiences that affect us deeply." As these experiences become even more meaningful, he explains, the corresponding brain changes gather even more momentum, in essence, building on themselves. Such experiences might involve drugs or alcohol: "Alcohol and heroin would certainly be less addictive, and a lot cheaper, if they led to experiences that were boring," Lewis writes.[6] But doesn't the process of falling in love, or the pursuit of excellence in sports, art, or business, also count as the motivated repetition of something special? Surely these pursuits can be equally as enthralling as a drug-induced high. And even though the outcomes of pursuits like these may be drastically different from drinking or doing drugs, what's happening inside our brains is very much the same; we're getting hooked on a powerful feeling. As we'll discuss in a few pages, the line between what we consider a destructive addiction and a productive passion is a fine one, if such a line exists at all.

THE SCIENCE BEHIND THE BIOLOGY OF PASSION IS COMpelling, but it is also young. Our understanding of the exact biochemical mechanisms underlying passion may change over time as the science progresses. Even so, there is enough evidence to believe that the overarching message is here to stay: A part of what we experience as passion is rooted in our genetic code and amplified by our neurochemistry. Some of us may be born with a persistent disposition, yet all of us can get hooked on the repetition of meaningful activities, whether this means seeing progress in training for a marathon, learning to play guitar, building a company, accelerating in one's career, or falling deeper into a romantic relationship. When we experience an intense urge to pursue something or someone, dopamine is flooding our brain, causing us to feel

> The line between what we consider a destructive addiction and a productive passion is a fine one, if such a line exists at all.

good in the moment and making us want to come back for more in the future. It is in this manner that passion builds on itself.

A compelling story, yes. But a complete one? Not quite. While our hereditary nature is important, so, too, is our nurture, or our life's experiences. Our DNA expresses itself differently based on the myriad of environmental factors to which we are exposed. Identical twins might carry the same genetic code, but almost always go on to live distinct lives with differing degrees of passion. In order to more fully understand what gives rise to the feeling of passion, then, we must look not just to biology but to psychology, too.

PASSION PRACTICES

- Passion is fueled by a neurochemical called dopamine.
- Dopamine doesn't make us feel good or content once we've achieved something; it makes us crave the chase.
- Some of us are born with an insensitivity to dopamine, thus predisposing us to feelings of passion and obsession.
- We are all, however, affected by the biology of passion. The more we pursue an activity that offers meaningful rewards, the more dopamine is released, leading us to build up a resistance over time.
- There is a biological reason why the wonderful feeling of passion cannot coexist with the wonderful feeling of contentment. Passion builds on itself: the more we push, the more we get hooked on the feeling of pushing.

SOMETHING TO PROVE:
THE PSYCHOLOGY OF PASSION

In 2009, endurance athlete Rich Roll was named by *Men's Fitness* as "one of the twenty-five fittest men in the world."[7] But unlike the ultrarunner Ann Trason, Roll wasn't always buzzing with endless energy; nor did he find himself obsessively gravitating toward any single pursuit as a kid. If anything, Roll was soft-spoken and shy, and carried himself with a calm demeanor. He was also an outsider. "I grew up kind of lonely," he tells us. "I didn't ever fully fit in. I look back and think at that time [during my childhood], I had all these doubts. I really wanted to prove myself, both to myself and to the outside world."

Roll was raised in a goal-oriented family. "Drive and achievement were an ethos in my household," he remembers. Even though he performed well academically, eventually earning acceptance to Stanford University, he felt that he never quite lived up to his parents' expectations. "The bar was just really high all the time, and I felt like I could never really reach it." In addition to his early academic "struggles," Roll struggled socially as well. "I was just an all-around extremely awkward young kid," he explains. "Picked last for kickball, wore braces and headgear, had a patch on one eye, was bullied on the playground, had difficulty learning. You get the point."

Put yourself in the shoes of nine-year-old Roll, and it's easy to see how he might have felt like he just wasn't good enough. But that all started to change in middle school, when Roll gave swimming a shot and immediately showed promise. "I wouldn't say I was a total natural, but yeah, it was clear that I was strong in the water," he recalls. Finally, after years of insecurity and self-doubt, Roll had discovered a venue in which he could excel. We asked Roll to try to remember what he was thinking when he first started swimming competitively. "Swimming was a chance to define myself," he answered, "to show that I, too, could succeed."[8]

First in and last out of the water throughout high school, Roll became hooked, developing an intimate relationship with the black line at the bottom of the pool. He swam, and swam, and swam. Thousands of training hours later, he was recruited to swim for Stanford, and after struggling with less healthy addictions—a common theme in passionate individuals—he became one of the best endurance athletes on the planet, completing events like the Ultraman, a 320-mile triathlon. It was as if Roll's childhood insecurities served as a pile of wood, and swimming was the spark to ignite a future of fiery passion. Might Roll's story have broader implications?

Professor Alan St Clair Gibson, PhD, MD, of the University of Essex in the UK, thinks so. Gibson specializes in integrative neuroscience. He's devoted much of his life to thinking about the intersection of mind and body. Gibson believes that passion may be rooted at least partially in something that Sigmund Freud long ago called ego fragility. In order to block out damaging events from one's past, Gibson says, people repress bad memories and experiences, relegating them deep into the subconscious. But these emotions can only stay bottled up for so long. Eventually, according to Gibson, they are "released through external drives or desires, often manifesting as energy put forth toward an unrelated activity." A telltale sign of this transference, Gibson says, is "fanatical attachment to projects and goals."[9]

Gibson is well aware that Freudian psychology has fallen out of favor, but the notion of ego fragility—that damaging events from one's past and insecurities can fuel later and seemingly unrelated obsessions—is supported by a wealth of more modern science. For instance, researchers from the University of Central Lancashire, in Preston, England, found that many top performers who exemplified relentless drive had also experienced adversity and discomfort—what the researchers call trauma—in their early years. Athletes who make it to the highest level of their respective sports, for example, tend to have a greater number of siblings (increased competition for their parents' attention) and are significantly more likely to have divorced parents. Out of this body of work came the increasingly popular phrase "talent needs trauma."[10]

"Trauma," of course, lies in the eyes of the beholder. The death of a parent or imprisonment of a sibling certainly registers as trauma, but so, too, might being bullied in grade school or never being invited to hang out with the "cool kids." Anything that someone experiences as disruptive, as fracturing their sense of self, could work to precipitate future passion and drive. "Trauma from times past," says Gibson, "creates an inner-mongrel which refuses to give up until the 'prize' is won."[11]

Although such trauma often comes from one's distant past, that need not be the case. Look at technology mogul Jim Clark: "I was thirty-eight years old. I'd just been fired. My second wife had just left me. I had somehow fucked up. I developed this maniacal passion for wanting to achieve *something*."[12] In mid-life, after going through a series of traumatic events, Clark's spark had been lit. He directed his passion toward emerging technologies, and it wasn't long before his "inner-mongrel" went on to transform the Internet by founding Netscape, the first mass-market web browser. From there, Clark created other tech companies, becoming one of Silicon Valley's first billionaires and the topic of a Michael Lewis book.[13]

Talent needs trauma.

Clark's drive may have been ignited by a desire to prove himself, but once he got into the work, it was nearly impossible for him to step away, even after he achieved success. Clark isn't alone. Though this isn't always the case, some kind of perceived past trauma is common among passionate individuals, and not only for the biological reasons we discussed earlier in this chapter. In addition to triggering a cycle of dopamine dependence and the ensuing feeling of ceaseless yearning, the relentless pursuit of an objective can also serve as an escape. Throwing ourselves wholly into a passion shrinks our world, overshadowing whatever inner struggles we may be facing and making us feel comfortable and in control. Our obsessions become a refuge. Places where we can fill the voids created by other insufficiencies in our lives. A chance to flee from the chaos and quiet the noise.

> Natalie had found some kind of completion, injecting herself with warmth, well-being, with a comfort nobody could deny her. By following a conscientious, almost clinical sequence of steps, she would arrive in a world of contentment that relied on no one—and that no one could take away from her.

This passage, written by neuroscientist Marc Lewis, describes Natalie, a heroin addict.[14] But it could just as easily be describing Natalie the Olympic swimmer, artist, writer, start-up founder, or computer programmer. It's not surprising that so many great athletes, creatives, and entrepreneurs, following their retirement, struggle with substance abuse and gambling addiction. If we don't move on from our passions thoughtfully (a topic we'll discuss later on), the same underlying biology and psychology that give rise to excellent pursuits can also give rise to harmful ones. Passion and addiction are close cousins.

It's worth taking a moment to note that the relationship between passion and addiction isn't always destructive. Consider a new program called Preventure, developed by Patricia Conrod, a professor of psychiatry at the University of Montreal. Preventure attempts to take advantage of the link between addiction and passion by identifying youth whose personality traits classify them as "at risk" for drug addiction and then intervening early with nonjudgmental school-based counseling. Among other goals, the counseling sessions help the students channel their "addictive personalities" toward productive activities.[15] A 2013 study of over 2,600 thirteen- and fourteen-year-olds across twenty-one British schools found that Preventure cut the risk of binge drinking by 43 percent among those enrolled in the program. For children with personality traits that put them at risk, this program is a godsend, altering their trajectory from future addict to up-and-coming entrepreneur or athlete.[16]

"When starving, when in love, and when parenting, being able to persist despite negative consequences—the essence of addictive behavior—is not a bug, but a feature, as programmers say. It can be the difference between life and death, between success and failure," writes psychology and neuroscience journalist Maia Szalavitz in her book *Unbroken Brain*. "However, when brain pathways intended to promote [positive attributes] are diverted into addiction, their blessings become curses. Love and addiction are alterations of the same brain circuits."[17]

The behaviors society condemns versus the behaviors society celebrates are often driven by many of the same underlying factors. And those same underlying factors that can lead to life-giving passions can easily go haywire and contribute to life-sapping addictions and even illnesses. Whether it's Trason and her hyperactive personality, Roll and his childhood struggles, or the at-risk youth in the Preventure program, individuals we praise for passion—who go on to experience huge successes—are often those who have a found a way to turn what could be seen as biological and psychological weaknesses into strengths, to control and harness these forces for good. This is something that we, Brad and Steve, are intimately aware of and constantly working toward in ourselves. The same drive, passion, and obsessive thinking that have led to many of our accomplishments—including this book—have also manifested in some of our lowest and most scary experiences. Brad is in ongoing recovery for obsessive-compulsive disorder (OCD), which, at its worst, takes him to the depths of indescribable darkness and is utterly debilitating. Meanwhile, Steve, though never formally diagnosed, used to feel compelled to complete certain tasks (i.e., touch doorknobs or turn an alarm on and off a specific number of times) before key track meets when he was atop the world in running. It's worth reiterating: The line between what is good and bad—between what is productive and destructive, between when lots of dopamine fuels generative action and when it leads to disorder—is a fine and fragile one.

BY NOW, A MORE COMPREHENSIVE PICTURE OF PASSION is beginning to emerge. At first, the *word* passion—at the time *passio*—implied suffering. Only more recently did it take on positive connotations. Yet depending on the circumstances, both definitions are still apt. The *feeling* of passion comes from both our evolutionary ancestors (nature) and our lived experiences (nurture). When we throw ourselves into an obsession, we attack deep-seated insecurities, fill voids from our past, and

---

Passion Practices

- Passion has not only biological roots, but psychological ones, too.
- The subjective feeling of struggle or "trauma" can be channeled into productive passions.
- Passionate pursuits often become psychological refuges, allowing you to hide from areas of your life that may be lacking: this can be both productive (keeps you from turning to destructive behaviors) and at the same time damaging (keeps you from confronting underlying issues).
- The same fundamental biology and psychology that give rise to passion also give rise to addiction; that's why it is so important to proactively channel these drives in yourself and those you nurture.

---

escape from things we may not want to face in our present. Our biology, and in particular a neurochemical called dopamine, fuels the pursuit. It keeps us coming back for more and prevents us from becoming content. Some of us may be born with a biological profile that makes us more likely to fall under passion's spell, but with enough repetition of an activity we view as meaningful, anyone can get hooked.

The rest of this book is about how to find something worthy of getting hooked on, and what happens when you do; and in particular, how you can develop the good kind of passion and harness and channel it in positive directions. Chapter 3 explores how to find or reaffirm your passion: how to turn your talents and interests into engaging, life-giving pursuits. Chapter 4 examines the dark, bad passion: the ways in which even a seemingly productive pursuit can become destructive. Becoming aware of these pitfalls will help you spot them in your own life so you can correct them early on. Chapter 5 examines the other (and far more desirable) passion, detailing the mind-set you must adopt in order to harness your passion and channel it in fruitful directions. You'll learn about the role of your outlook and ego in determining which path your passion takes, as well as practical tools you can employ to ensure your passion remains harmonious with the rest of your life. Chapter 6 turns to the question of whether a passionate person can achieve "balance." Is it possible to master the relentless pursuit of an activity while at the same time holding on to other joys in life? Should you even try? How can you fiercely pursue a passion without burning out? Chapter 7 focuses on the power of self-awareness—why it is the key to sustaining passion for a lifetime and how to cultivate it in yourself. Finally, in chapter 8, you'll learn how you can move on from a passion with both grace and grit. It is our hope that you walk away from this book with a richer and more nuanced understanding of passion. And, far more important, that you walk away from this book with a better sense of how to deliberately manage passion in your own life—so your relationship with passion will always be a gift, never a curse.

> *Individuals we praise for passion—who go on to experience huge successes—are often those who have a found a way to turn what could be seen as biological and psychological weaknesses into strengths.*

3

Find and Grow Your Passion

Since the beginning of documented history, humans have tried to understand the consuming sensations underlying love. Philosophers, artists, poets, and scientists have all provided their respective takes—ranging from the metaphysical to the spiritual to the biochemical. As children, we are told stories of love and romantic passion, fairy tales about finding Prince Charming and fables filled with advice on how we'll know when we've found *the one*: It will be an immediate attraction; we'll feel it deep down in our guts; we won't be able to stop thinking about said person. We're told that if we can just find our one true love, all our sorrows will fade away. Our frustrations will vanish as our soul mate accepts us for who we are and makes up for our own imperfections. If only we can find our one true love, the story goes, we'll experience satisfaction and bliss.

The concept of a singular love is thoroughly etched into most of our minds. Although it may have been decades since we last watched cartoons with Disney heroes searching for their true loves, many people have not let go of the idea that there is a single "right" person for them. In one survey conducted by the Marist Institute for Public Opinion, 73 percent of people stated they believe in a soul mate.[1]

It wasn't always this way. The term *soul mate* didn't become popular until the beginning of the twentieth century. Before then, our ideas about love and marriage were far more nuanced, and perhaps far more practical, too. Throughout most of history, love dealt with not just raw emotion, but also reason. People commonly got married for business, familial, or other pragmatic purposes. The notion that enduring love need not always manifest as an immediate and powerful attraction traces itself all the way back to the ancient Greeks, who viewed love as a practice of continually learning about and growing closer to one's partner—more a process of cultivation than an instant connection. Instead of being preoccupied with *searching* for the perfect match, for centuries, people *worked to develop* intimate bonds over time.

But with the rise of Romanticism in the nineteenth century—a period that prized emotional feeling over cognitive thinking—the prevailing attitude toward love began to shift. The Romantics believed that the emotions and sensations you experience should be the guide, reason be damned. Love became a quest to find an overpowering feeling, an instant magnetism indicating that one has found their one and only match. Social scientists refer to this mind-set as "the destiny belief of love," and it remains the prevailing one today.

What are the consequences of such a mind-set? For starters, researchers have found that those who subscribe to a destiny belief system of love are more likely to end relationships when the first hint of conflict occurs; in essence, they decide, *This person must not be the one*, and move on in search of someone who *is* the one.[2] That's because under a destiny belief of love mind-set, the need to choose the perfect match is paramount: If you do not choose correctly, the thinking goes, there is little you can do to alter your course; if you're not fully confident that you've found your one and only soul mate, you've effectively settled for a lesser match. Unfortunately, the destiny belief system of love is often misguided. It is very much an all-or-nothing approach, and far too often leaves people on a never-ending search for some sort of illusory perfection.

The way in which we view love affects not only how we pursue our romantic relationships, but also how we pursue our passions. As we touched on in the previous chapter, passion and love have a deep and intertwined relationship. So it should not be surprising that when it comes to finding a passion, much like with love, the prevailing wisdom is that we ought to search for the perfect fit. There is an expectation that the initial alchemy, the feeling we have when we start a new hobby or job, should send a clear signal as to whether we've hit the mark: We should be excited, enthusiastic, and energized. If we don't experience these positive emotions from the get-go, best to keep on searching.

In the small but growing world of passion research, this is called a "fit mind-set" of passion, and it very much parallels the destiny belief system of love. According to the latest research, 78 percent of individuals hold a fit mind-set, meaning they believe happiness comes from finding an activity or job about which they are immediately passionate, something that feels intuitively right from the get-go.[3]

While this mind-set may be the most prevalent one, it's not necessarily best. Individuals who adopt a fit mind-set of passion tend to overemphasize their initial feelings. They are more likely to choose pursuits (and especially professions) based on preliminary assessments, not potential for growth—even though the latter is generally more important than the former for lasting fulfillment and satisfaction. People with fit mind-sets for passion are also more likely to give up on new pursuits at the first sign of challenge or disappointment, shrugging their shoulders and thinking, *I guess this isn't for me.* Furthermore, studies show that individuals with fit mind-sets actually expect their passions to dwindle over time, setting themselves up for midlife crises once their initial enthusiasm for an activity has diminished.[4] Put all this together, and a compelling story emerges: A fit mind-set for passion is constraining; it inherently limits one to activities that feel good immediately and makes one fragile to challenge or change.

This isn't to say you should ignore the initial excitement that may come with new ideas and activities when you are trying to find a passion. But you shouldn't be so fixated on finding something that feels perfect from the outset, either. Much like the mind-set of perfect love at first sight often leaves people without love, the mind-set of perfect passion at first encounter often leaves people without passion. A better approach to finding your passion is to lower the bar from perfect to interesting, then give yourself permission to pursue your interests with an open mind.

Take the decision to create one of history's highest-grossing movies of all time, *Titanic.* As director James Cameron told *Men's Journal,* he didn't set out with the knowledge or goal of

> *A better approach to finding your passion is to lower the bar from perfect to interesting, then give yourself permission to pursue your interests with an open mind.*

creating one of the biggest blockbuster films to date. He had simpler ambitions: "I don't think the studio executives believed it, but I wanted to make *Titanic* because I wanted to dive the wreck. I thought: How can I dive the

Titanic and get somebody to pay for it? I'll make a movie." Cameron was simply pursuing his interest; the end product, perhaps the most popular movie of all time, was an afterthought. As Cameron told *Men's Journal*, it was a side effect of a "personal quest."

Or consider Marissa Neuman, a thirty-two-year-old PhD student of philosophy at the University of Texas. Over a decade ago, Neuman studied philosophy as an undergraduate student. But like so many other people who study philosophy as undergraduates, she convinced herself (and was convinced by others) that it would be impossible to make a living as a philosopher—so she went to law school.

At law school, Neuman's interest was always, and almost exclusively, piqued by philosophy courses. In her spare time, she wasn't reading legal reviews or popular industry blogs like *Above the Law*. She was reading philosophy. After three years of school and adding a JD to her name, Neuman decided practicing as an attorney would leave her dissatisfied and unfulfilled. But she still had student loan debt to pay off and felt unsure of how to make a life out of philosophy. So she went out into the work world, holding jobs in advertising and nonprofit development and fund-raising.

Though on its face it seemed like Neuman had strayed not only from the law, but also from philosophy, in reality she was continuing to pursue her interest: "The parts of my jobs I loved most, and how I crafted my jobs, was to have the big strategic conversations, to be involved in asking and trying to answer the big questions: Why are we doing what we're doing? How should we go about accomplishing our purpose?" Some of her colleagues might have thought she was trying to get in front of upper management so she could get promoted. But that wasn't the case at all. "I just wanted to have these big conversations, and [with management] was the place to have them," she recalls. In the meantime, when she wasn't at work, she continued to read philosophy and seek out philosophical conversations in her free time. She kept an open mind, never closing herself off to philosophy, but never considering it her one and only calling either.

"At no point during this process did I think to myself, 'I'll just keep these jobs and pay off my debt and then figure out how to make it in philosophy,'" she says. "I was just letting my curiosity take me forward and engaging in the things I enjoyed and found interesting." Fast-forward five years, and Neuman had paid off her law school debt (she was fortunate to have received a scholarship, so the debt wasn't *that* massive) and found herself applying to PhD programs in philosophy. "In hindsight," she says, "it seems like I had this grand plan, from the time I was eighteen and just starting as an undergraduate. But that's not the case at all. I was just following my interests and the path unfolded in front of me."

"Interest" is really just another way of saying that something captures your attention. When you come across an activity or idea that subtly pulls you toward it, you are faced with a choice: Do you grant yourself permission to lean in and further explore? Or do you let it go, ignoring it and writing it off as a momentary blip of intrigue? If you choose to ignore, you send a strong message—and one that quickly gets encoded in your brain—that the activity or idea carries little value. The next time you encounter something similar, your brain won't send a signal for excitement; it will have already gotten the message that "there's nothing to pursue here." If, however, you engage during moments of initial intrigue, your brain will do the opposite, hardwiring a neural connection that says, "It's worth my energy and focus to pursue the things that interest me."

PASSION PRACTICES

- Take a moment to reflect on your mind-set around passion. Do you hold a "fit mind-set"? If so, you're not alone: Research shows that over 78 percent of people believe happiness comes from finding a hobby or job that they are passionate about from the outset.
- It's important to beware of the pitfalls of a fit mind-set for passion:
  - You're more likely to give up on new pursuits at the first sign of challenge or discomfort.
  - You're more likely to sacrifice opportunities for long-term growth and development in favor of fleeting short-term pleasures.
  - You're more likely to succumb to "midlife crises" as the activities you engage in evolve over time.
  - You're less likely to find a lasting passion because you bounce from one not-quite-perfect endeavor to the next.
- Especially when first exploring new ideas and activities, don't let perfect be the enemy of good.
- Select "interesting" over "perfect." Having an open mind and playfully exploring your interests is better than trying to find something that immediately feels perfect.

Interest is an invitation to exploration, drawing your attention toward activities that have the potential to grow into something greater. But that can only occur if you accept the invitation.[5]

Unfortunately, far too often when a feeling of intrigue or

curiosity arises, we simply let it go. In some cases, we tell our-selves we're too busy, quickly becoming distracted by our smartphones or the next item on our to-do list. Other times, we tell ourselves that wherever an initial spark of intrigue is lead-ing must not be for us because it conflicts with our perceived identity; a form of resistance that we call "I couldn't possibly do this" syndrome. Common examples of "I couldn't possibly do this" syndrome include: "I went to and paid for business school, why should I be concerned with art?" "I'm a physician, not an essay writer." "I'm sixty-four years old and I've never worked with my hands, why start now?"

"I couldn't possibly do this" syndrome only grows stronger with age. It also creates a formidable sense of path dependency, or the narrative that you are on a certain path, and the best—if not only—option is to stay on it. But path dependency prevents you from exploring opportunities that could lead to a better and more fulfilling life. You'll never know if you're truly on the right path unless you allow yourself to explore and pursue the things that capture your attention, even if they seem to conflict with the current path or identity you've constructed for yourself. You must resist the temptation to pigeonhole yourself into any one box, regardless of your prior experiences. Just think about how many potential passions are killed by close-mindedness, by prematurely telling yourself that an activity or idea is not worth your attention before you've even explored it to a sufficient degree.

Interest is an invitation to exploration, drawing your attention toward activities that have the potential to grow into something greater.

Embracing exploration is so important because the path to finding your passion can be long and circuitous, with many wrong turns in the direction of activities, jobs, or other opportunities that initially appeared exhilarating yet proved to be something else. But have the courage to keep on exploring. This doesn't mean you should pursue just anything and everything, but it does mean you should nurture an open mind, and not move on so swiftly from the activities and ideas that capture your attention. Be wary of fully embracing a fit mindset for passion, stopping any activity that doesn't feel *perfect* right off the bat. Instead, give yourself the freedom

You must resist the temptation to pigeonhole yourself into any one box, regardless of your prior experiences.

to explore budding interests enough to more accurately judge if they could grow into passions, a potential that often depends on whether a pursuit satisfies three basic needs.

PASSION PRACTICES

- When an idea or activity interests you, give yourself permission to pursue it.
- Don't be constrained by the story you tell yourself about yourself, or by your past experiences.
- Overcome the resistance that is "I couldn't possibly do this" syndrome and allow moments of intrigue to capture your attention, even if they seem divergent from your current path.
- Remember that nearly all grand passions began as someone merely following their interests.

SATISFYING OUR BASIC NEEDS

In the early 1970s, psychologists Edward Deci and Richard Ryan developed a concept called self-determination theory that forever changed how the scientific community viewed motivation. Deci and Ryan found that, contrary to common wisdom (both then and, to a large extent, now), one's drive to pursue activities is *not* predominantly reliant on external rewards like money, fame, or recognition. Rather, enduring motivation comes from satisfying three basic needs: competency, autonomy, and relatedness.[6]

1. **Competency** is about having a sense of control over the outcome of your efforts and the ability to make progress over time. If you don't believe that your efforts will be rewarded with improvement, why put forth any effort to begin with? If you don't feel like you're progressing in an activity—be it better performance, more enjoyment, or some other measure of "success"—then why continue? Competency fills an innate human desire for tangible progress linked back to one's actions. If you put in the work, you want to get something out of it.

2. **Autonomy,** also sometimes referred to as *authenticity*, is about acting in harmony with your innermost being. It means you're connecting what you do with who you are. Your work should reflect your core values and beliefs; you should express some part of your innermost self in your activity. Unfortunately, in a modern economy that emphasizes external rewards over internal fulfillment, too many have lost sight of this basic need. And yet researchers from the University of Washington have found that autonomy is absolutely critical to lasting passion and happiness:

The great benefit of being able to convincingly rationalize one's work as a manifestation of the true self is that it gives the individual direction and purpose. Work then provides answers to an individual's fundamental questions: "Who am I?" and "What should I do with my life?"[7]

When you are exploring new interests, ask yourself if they reflect your core values. Perhaps they allow you to express creativity and freedom, or to grow wisdom and strength. These are just a few examples. Core values are highly personal. The point is that you should take a moment to have an intimate conversation with yourself. What do you really stand for? Do your outward activities reflect your inner self? Too many people fly through life without making time for this sort of reflection. Yet it is this very kind of reflection that ensures you spend your time in a meaningful way.

3. **Relatedness:** The final component of self-determination theory is one that binds us to others: the need to feel connected to and/or like you are a part of something larger. Humans are social animals. Our ability to work together in highly integrated groups and to display empathy toward one another helped our species thrive and grow over multiple millennia. Cooperation—whether it was taking care of young, protecting territory, or hunting and gathering food for the group instead of just for oneself—allowed for survival at a much higher rate. The need to feel connected to others and rooted in a larger whole is literally programmed into our DNA.

    This doesn't always mean that the best jobs and activities are those performed in groups, but it does mean that you're more likely to stick with something that makes you feel like you are a part of something greater. There are many ways to achieve this: Are you working with others? Does your work touch others? Is your work a continuation of what others have done before you? Is your work setting the stage for others to build upon? Does your work make you part of a community, be it a physical or intellectual one? Whatever form the connection takes, that connection is critical.

If an activity meets these needs, you're exponentially more likely to enjoy it and stick with it. Satisfying these three needs is almost always required for enduring passion to take hold.

Activities that fulfill these three basic needs are the ones we should throw ourselves into. Engaging in such activities gives us the best chance to bring about one of the most rewarding feelings there is: a feeling of aliveness and self-actualization, that you're doing exactly what you're meant to be doing. The emergence of such a feeling is a telltale sign of blossoming passion. When you begin to experience such a feeling, the temptation is to fully dive in. Yet, as you'll soon see, that would be a mistake. Because the best way to fully develop passion is gradually.

MAKE YOUR PASSION A BIGGER PART OF YOUR LIFE—INCREMENTALLY

Once you've begun to cultivate an emerging passion, it's only a matter of time before you're liable to ask yourself some simple yet significant questions: *How can I spend more of my time and energy pursuing this new passion? How can I make it a bigger part of my life? What if I want to go "all in"? When will I know I'm ready?* In her book *The Crossroads of Should and Must: Find*

PASSION PRACTICES

- Finding your passion can feel like a long and winding path, but there is a road map to make the process easier:
  - Don't let perfect be the enemy of good: Resist the urge to assign too much importance to the initial excitement that comes with starting a new job, activity, or hobby. If you expect a perfect match from the outset, odds are, you'll be let down.
  - Pay special attention to activities that meet your three basic needs: competence, autonomy, and relatedness. Meeting these needs is critical to sustaining the motivation required to turn an interest into a passion.

and Follow Your Passion, the artist and writer Elle Luna makes a strong case for fast and full immersion. Luna believes that far too many people stick to their "should"—the safe route; their comfort zone and usual routine; what they feel they ought to be doing and what is expected of them. She wishes more people would have the courage to pursue their "must," or the thing that truly excites them and makes them come alive. Luna urges readers who have found a passion to chase after it, to throw themselves into it and not look back.[8] Luna's far from alone in her sentiment. Go to any bookstore and browse the titles about passion. They tend to share a common theme: Dive into your budding passion with reckless abandon.

For Luna, throwing herself completely into her passion meant leaving her job at a software start-up to make art. Her decision proved to be a good one. She authored a bestselling book and now spends her time painting, designing, and writing. She was able, as she puts it, to "choose must." This is a choice that many people assume is required to get on a new path, to chase their dreams and bring them to fruition. Yet "choosing must" isn't always possible, or wise. Not everyone has the risk tolerance, practical ability, or financial security to make such a choice, to suddenly quit their job or upend other areas of their life to wholly pursue an emerging passion. And yet it turns out that's actually OK. It might even be

Once you've begun to cultivate an emerging passion, it's only a matter of time before you're liable to ask yourself some simple yet significant questions: How can I spend more of my time and energy pursuing this new passion? How can I make it a bigger part of my life?

advantageous. Because the best route to making your passion a bigger part of your life is often *not* to choose must *over* should, but rather to choose must *and* should.

Consider "Should I Quit My Day Job? A Hybrid Path to Entrepreneurship," a recent investigation published in the *Academy of Management Journal*. For the study, a pair of University of Wisconsin researchers set out to answer what, in the age of start-ups, has become a common question: If you want to do something entrepreneurial—in essence, attempting to monetize a passion—are you better off keeping or quitting your day job? After interviewing thousands of entrepreneurs, they found that those who kept their day job while pursuing a personal venture on the side—or what the researchers called "hybrid entrepreneurship"—were 33 percent *less* likely to fail than those who quit their jobs altogether.[9] As the *Harvard Business Review* put it, "Going all-in on your start-up might not be the best idea."[10]

Going all in on something makes you fragile, especially if you go all in prematurely. Pressure to perform, be it financial or psychological, often leads you away from thoughtfulness and logic and toward a more irrational style of decision-making. When you go all in, you move from a place of *wanting* to succeed to *needing* to succeed. As the well-known Oakland Athletics' baseball executive Billy Beane bluntly points out, "The day you say you have to do something, you're screwed. Because you are going to make a bad deal."[11] Instead of backing yourself into such a corner, perhaps the better move is to adopt what author and investor Nassim Taleb calls a "barbell strategy." The image of a barbell—two weights on opposite ends—symbolizes stability. One side of the barbell characterizes low-risk, low-reward scenarios, whereas the opposite side characterizes high-risk, high-reward scenarios. It represents what Taleb calls "a dual attitude of playing it safe in some areas and taking risks in others," all the while avoiding the middle ground that is neither completely safe nor carries a big payoff.[12]

The best route to making your passion a bigger part of your life is often not to choose must over should, but rather to choose must and should.

Such a strategy brings two major benefits: First, you are more likely to take bigger risks with higher payoffs when you know that failure won't ruin you. You won't have to worry about playing it safe or constantly second-guessing yourself while pursuing your passion. Second, even if you initially come up short, you'll still be OK (thanks to maintaining your stable gig) and thus you can continue using different strategies to try to make your passion a bigger part of your life. In other words, the barbell strategy says that you should pursue your passion incrementally. Doing so relieves pressure and allows more room for error. It affords you the chance to fail and to learn from

Going all in on something makes you fragile, especially if you go all in prematurely.

your failures. Though pursuing your passion in such a manner may feel painstakingly dull in the short run, it increases your chances of being successful in the long run. Those who go big or go home often end up going home. Those who go incrementally over a long period of time often end up with something big. The best route to making your passion a bigger part of your life is to do so gradually.

Brad knows the barbell strategy well. He's followed it (and still does) pretty much to a T while turning his passion for writing and coaching into a profession. For Brad, "should" is a corporate consulting job. It pays well; most of the work is in healthcare and he finds it meaningful; he gets to partner with high-ranking executives; and he likes the people with whom he works. Yet ever since he was a kid, for Brad "must" was always writing (and this was even after getting rejected by Northwestern University's prestigious Medill School of Journalism) and one-on-one coaching. So even amid a busy consulting job, he wrote regularly on a personal blog and coached a handful of people. Eventually, some of his blog posts were noticed, which led to a few professional opportunities. When he had his first major column published in the *Los Angeles Times* in 2013 and soon after started landing more prestigious freelance gigs, he was tempted to quit his day job.[13] But he didn't. Instead, he continued to write on the side. Sure, as the writing and coaching continued to pick up, he went down in consulting hours, but he never quit; he never went "all in" on writing and coaching. To this day, two published books and an executive coaching practice later, Brad still consults part-time.

The barbell strategy allowed Brad to be more selective about

> *Those who go big or go home often end up going home. Those who go incrementally over a long period of time often end up with something big.*

what and for whom he writes and whom he coaches. It also made him a better writer. It left him more relaxed and enabled him to focus on quality; he didn't need to churn out a bunch of clickbait articles to pay rent. It also gave him the confidence to take shots he otherwise might not have taken because he knew

The best route to making your passion a bigger part of your life is to do so gradually.

that failure was, in fact, a not so bad outcome. Does Brad long for the day when he can spend all his time writing and coaching? Absolutely. It's just that he's realized his best chance of getting (and staying) there is to do so incrementally, gradually shifting the balance of his time and energy—and, most pragmatically, his income—to those passions. When Brad first began following this strategy over eight years ago, his personal balance was around 99 percent consulting, 1 percent writing and coaching. Now it's gradually approaching the opposite.

There is, of course, a case to be made for going all in on a passion from the outset, for choosing must *over* should. Perhaps for those who truly thrive under immense pressure, going all in from the outset translates to better performance. But for the vast majority of people—at least according to the research—the best route to directing more time and energy toward a passion is to follow the barbell strategy, incrementally shifting more and more weight away from safe and stable (i.e., your day job) and toward what makes you tick (i.e., your passion). In *The Crossroads of Should and Must,* Elle Luna tells the story of international-bestselling author John Grisham, who started off as a "lawyer/author," awaking every day at five a.m. "to write stories about harrowing crimes and evil doings all before going to his job at the courthouse." It was only after three years of juggling writing and criminal defense that Grisham shaped his stories into a novel, which, after multiple rejections, was finally accepted for publication. And *that*, Luna writes, "is why John Grisham is a household name today."[14] In other words, for quite some time, Grisham didn't choose must *over* should. He chose must *and* should.

And yet ending there would be finishing Grisham's story prematurely. He didn't stay in his job as a lawyer forever. At a certain point, he *did* make the choice to go all in on writing. Over thirty bestselling books later, his choice certainly looks like a good one. This highlights an important point: Pursuing your passion incrementally gets you pretty far—ironically, at least according to the research out of Harvard, farther than if you'd gone all in from the outset. For lots of people, this is far enough. Doing what you love as a hobby or side-gig is quite fulfilling and carries minimal risk. But if you are determined to fully live out your passion—to truly devote your all to it, to make it the centerpiece of your life—at a certain point you've got to make a bet on yourself. You've got to take a leap of faith and go all in.

GOING ALL IN

There's an old Buddhist saying that faith is the confidence born out of realizing the fruits of practice. "It is like the confidence a farmer has in his way of growing crops," writes the Zen master Thich Nhat Hanh. "This kind of faith is not blind. It is not some belief in a set of ideas or dogmas."[15] *This* is the kind of faith that is required to quit your job, or move across the country, or go back to school to fully pursue your passion. It's not the kind of faith that is based on a premonition or gut feeling. It's the kind of faith that is based on an expansive body of evidence, evidence that you've provided for yourself; that you've put in the work and have the skills; that you've cultivated your passion incrementally for long enough and have what is required to take it to the next level. Though success in pursuing a passion full-on is never guaranteed, its probability increases when you can respond to the following prompts—key pieces of evidence, if you will—in the affirmative:

- I've done the work that is necessary to put myself in a position to thrive.
- I've tested my current skills multiple times and know they are sufficient to at least stay afloat (financially, physically, emotionally) when I jump in.
- I have the desire and work ethic to continue developing my skills.
- I've reflected on the sacrifices I'll need to further pursue my passion, and I'm OK making them.
- I have a plan of action, including mentors, the support of family and friends, and specific progression markers or milestones to shoot for. I'm also willing to adapt my plan if need be.
- I may feel a little jittery, but the thought of going all in on my passion does *not* make me anxious. It makes me excited.
- I *want* to do this, and I'm committed to everything this encompasses.

If you found yourself nodding your head to each of the above bullets and you believe you're ready to go all in on your passion (or, if you're already pursuing your passion, to stay on the path), then this is the kind of faith that supports such a decision. If you're still unsure about any of the above, that's OK, too. It just means you should probably continue pursuing your passion incrementally until you become more confident, until you give yourself *more reason* to have faith. There's no way to be 100 percent certain when the time is right to go all in, but when you have sufficient faith, making the leap won't be as scary. It won't even feel like that much of a leap. It will simply be taking the next logical step on your progression toward living life with more passion.

MOST PEOPLE THINK THAT ONCE THEY'VE IDENTIFIED and made their passion a big part of their lives, it's smooth sailing from there. A common trajectory goes like this: You find and cultivate your passion; you pursue it incrementally until you have the faith to go all in; you go all in (or damn near close), start crushing it, love your more passion-filled life, and perhaps even begin getting positive recognition for your accomplishments. At this point, everything is going great. But what you don't realize is that you're approaching a fine line, which, if you cross it, could put you in a pretty bad spot. Remember what you read at the outset of this book: Passion can be a gift, but it can also be a curse. If you're not careful and deliberate, the bad kind of passion—*passio*, suffering—will creep up on you without you even noticing. At best, you'll fight through it, but will have wasted precious energy that could have been better spent elsewhere. At worst, it will derail your passion, and possibly your entire life.

While countless stories end with how to find your passion, in reality, that's just the beginning. The harder part is learning how to live with it in a productive and sustainable manner. Before exploring how to nurture the best kind of passion, harmoniously integrate it into your life, and set yourself up for a smooth transition if you decide or are forced to move on from

Passion Practices

- The best way to make an emerging passion a bigger part of your life is to pursue it incrementally.
- Following the barbell strategy—that is, sticking to something safe on one hand while you increasingly take risks to pursue your passion on the other—increases the chances you'll succeed at making your passion a bigger part of your life.
  - You are more likely to take bigger and higher payoff risks when you know that failure won't ruin you.
  - Even if you initially come up short, you'll still be OK and thus can continue using different strategies to invest in your passion.
- Over time, gradually shift the equation, spending more time and energy pursuing your passion and less time on the "safer" stuff.
- At a certain point, you'll reach a position to decide whether it's time to go all in on your passion, to make some big changes so you can devote more of your life to it. This requires making a leap of faith.
- Remember: This kind of "faith" is not based on a premonition or gut feeling. It is based on confidence born out of realizing the fruits of practice. If you create a body of evidence that you'll be successful for yourself (see page 53), your leap won't seem like that much of a leap at all.

it (chapters 5 through 8), you must first gain an understanding of passion's dark side so that you can prevent it from taking root in your own life. Unfortunately, most people experience at least some semblance of passion's dark side prior to fully reaping passion's positive rewards. But this need not be the case. You can avoid passion's dark side. You just need to know what to look out for.

4

When Passion Goes Awry

One of history's most fiercely driven executives once said, "I value passion probably more than any other attribute."[1] As CEO of a $60 billion company, he saw to it that only the most passionate employees were recruited. He encouraged the pursuit of impeccable results at all costs and rewarded those who worked with unabashed fervor. Employees arrived early and stayed late, trading their biological families for their corporate one. Everyone, and especially those in senior positions, was incredibly passionate about performance. It was paying off. During his reign as CEO, his company was rated by *Fortune* as "the most innovative large company in America," and its stock dramatically outperformed the market.[2]

The CEO's name was Jeffrey Skilling. His company was Enron.

We're all aware of the fraud that poisoned the behemoth energy company under Skilling's leadership. It cost shareholders billions of dollars. Thousands of employees lost not only their jobs but also their life's savings, which were in many cases tied to now worthless company stock. Skilling's unadulterated passion to keep growing Enron's financial performance gave rise to the most monumental corporate fraud case and ensuing bankruptcy in history.

Only a few years later, a nineteen-year-old Stanford dropout who idolized Steve Jobs, and whose father happened to have worked for Skilling at Enron, launched a biotech company that she promised would change the world. The company grew at warp speed, attracting hundreds of millions of dollars in investments and landing partnerships with leaders in the health and wellness industry. Speaking to Maria Shriver at *Vanity Fair*'s New Establishment Summit in 2015, when asked what advice she'd give anyone wanting to start a company, the then thirty-one-year-old CEO harped on the importance of passion and obsession: "The purpose of school to me was always to learn the tools to be able to pursue what you love," she told Shriver. "And I felt like I had those tools to be able to now go obsess over what it was I wanted to be doing no matter what."[3]

The *Vanity Fair* summit was just one of many. This wildly successful CEO became a poster child for driven young people everywhere, attracting unprecedented media attention and gracing the cover of magazines like *Forbes, Inc., Fortune,* and *Bloomberg.* All these feature stories highlighted her obsessive pursuit of success. In late 2015, the *Washington Post* summarized her relentless drive: "Her success illustrates the importance of being obsessed if you want to launch a disruptive start-up."[4]

The *Post* got two things right. 1) Elizabeth Holmes was obsessed; and 2) Theranos, her biotech company, was insanely disruptive, only not in the positive way the *Post* had implied. Less than a year after Holmes gave her powerful interview on passion at the *Vanity Fair* summit, the same magazine covered her again, this time in a different light. The story, titled "How Elizabeth Holmes's House of Cards Came Tumbling Down," detailed the fall of Theranos.[5] The company—which promised a "world-changing," inexpensive, and less painful way to administer and analyze blood tests—had the federal government threatening sanctions for failing to meet performance standards and not providing sufficient evidence of efficacy, and also settled a lawsuit from leading investors accusing the company of securities fraud.[6,7] Right before this book went to print, Theranos and Holmes settled with the SEC for charges of "massive fraud" and Holmes was indicted for fraud by the federal government.[8] At its peak, Theranos was valued at $9 billion. Just a few years later, the company is dissolving.

OBSESSIVE PASSION

Skilling did not set out to destabilize an entire financial sector or to defraud the public, and Holmes initially wanted to do good science. Both began as brilliant, driven, and seemingly unblemished individuals. Skilling was a graduate of the Harvard Business School and started his career as one of the youngest management consultants at the illustrious firm McKinsey & Company. Holmes was a Stanford undergrad, intent on innovation and discovery and with countless patents to her name. No doubt their immense passion contributed to their early accolades. Yet it also led them astray. And although they are profound examples of what happens when passion goes awry, they aren't alone.

Similar fiascos occur on smaller scales all the time. Someone becomes overly fixated on achieving a goal, wrapping his identity in it and losing sight of his inner reasons for setting out to accomplish it in the first place. He becomes driven by the external rewards and recognition that he imagines accomplishing his goal will bring, and he goes to any extreme to achieve it. This disease manifests itself in many forms, including plagiarizing (*have to publish that book*); using banned performance-enhancing drugs (*must make the Olympic team*); or, like Skilling, partaking in fraudulent behavior in the workplace (*gotta hit sales targets or get that promotion*).

These are all telltale examples of what University of Quebec psychology professor Robert Vallerand calls obsessive passion. While nearly all passions can lead to feelings of obsession, Vallerand's obsessive passion refers to those that become motivated by achievement, results, and external rewards more so than by internal satisfaction. It's when someone becomes more passionate about *the rewards an activity might bring* than about doing the activity itself.

Obsessive passion can quickly hijack a joyful and righteous pursuit and turn it into a dark one. One of the foremost reasons for this is that someone who is obsessively passionate ties their self-worth to things outside their control. This often ends up creating high levels of distress.

- An athlete becomes passionate about—or, rather, obsessed with—finishing an Ironman triathlon in a certain amount of time. For six months he trains twenty hours every week, neglecting his family and friends. Unprecedented weather conditions strike on race day. If that wasn't enough, he has the misfortune of a flat tire during the bike portion of the race. His finishing time is far slower than he had hoped for.
- An associate at a law firm wants nothing more than to become partner. She works tirelessly in service of that goal and wraps her entire identity around one day sitting in a

corner office. Her boss who was going to promote her suddenly becomes ill and retires. She doesn't get promoted.

- A young writer craves being published. He imagines his name on the *New York Times* bestseller list. He pens what he believes to be a masterpiece. His manuscript is rejected by all the major publishing houses.

Are the subjects in these examples failures? If judged based on whether they achieved the result they were after, then, unfortunately, the answer is yes. Being passionate about—or, perhaps better put, a slave to—the achievement of an external result that you cannot control creates a volatile and fragile sense of self-worth.

This insight isn't exactly new. Nearly two thousand years ago, the Stoic philosopher Epictetus warned against becoming attached to what he called externals:

> Over and above the rest we have masters in the form of circumstances, which are legion. And anyone who controls any one of them controls us as well. When we love, hate, or fear such things, then the people [or circumstances] that administer them are bound to become our masters. Do not desire anything outside the limits of your authority. Don't let your hands go near it, much less your desire. Otherwise you've consigned yourself to slavery and submitted yourself to the yoke, as you do whenever you prize something not yours to command, or grow attached to something that's contingent on variable, unstable, unpredictable, and unreliable [factors].[9]

When our sense of self is tied to external results, desperation inevitably follows. Nearly all success includes at least some

Being passionate about—or, perhaps better put, a slave to—the achievement of an external result that you cannot control creates a volatile and fragile sense of self-worth.

degree of failure. If you can't accept those failures honestly, openly, and with humility, then fraud, angst, and depression are a likely path. That's because the experience of failure, or even just a lack of progress, becomes a personal attack. With every step backward or in the wrong direction, our ego, our literal sense of "self," takes a hit. When people speak poorly about our company or dislike our work, they aren't attacking an object or an output; they are attacking *us*. It's no wonder Skilling went to such an extreme to maintain the facade and Holmes got herself into such trouble. It is likely that they weren't protecting their companies; they were protecting themselves.

Years before Skilling's and Holmes's falls from grace, the late psychologist and humanist thinker Erich Fromm wrote, "Human freedom is restricted to the extent to which we are bound to our own egos. By being bound to our egos we stand in our own way . . . If I am what I have and if what I have is lost, then who am I?"[10] Fusing a large part of your identity with *any* external result is a dangerous game.

Even when people experience legitimate success (as both Skilling and Holmes did at first), if it is the outcome of obsessive passion—fueled by a longing for external results and rewards—they are bound for future trouble. Those who are most focused on reaching some external barometer of success are often the same people who struggle most to enjoy it. That's because they'll always crave more. More money. More fame. More medals. More followers. As discussed earlier in this book, once we become

Those who are most focused on reaching some external barometer of success are often the same people who struggle most to enjoy it.

passionate about something, our biology makes it nearly impossible for us to feel content, and our psychology only further attaches us to the pursuit. It becomes easy to get sucked into a vicious cycle. "Vicious," because eventually we'll experience a negative result. And when we do—well, you don't need us to tell you how that might feel.

Modern behavioral science has a phrase to describe this never-ending cycle of searching for satisfaction and self-worth founded in something that lies outside of our control: *hedonic adaptation*. Hedonic adaptation says that we quickly adapt to a state of happiness or contentedness, and it's not long before we'll want more. Centuries before hedonic adaptation became an academic concept, the Buddha also had a term for this never-ending pursuit of external success: He called it suffering.

"Our very success can be the cause of a greater anxiety for further preservation of our success," writes the poet David Whyte.[11] He's right. Researchers have found that regardless of the field, individuals who display obsessive passion are more likely to engage in unethical behavior and are at a higher risk for anxiety, depression, and burnout. Their relationship with their passion is likely to erode, and their overall life satisfaction is poor. Still, some, like Skilling and Holmes, will go to great lengths to keep the cycle going. And this holds true far beyond the boardroom.

> *Hedonic adaptation says that we quickly adapt to a state of happiness or contentedness, and it's not long before we'll want more. The Buddha called this suffering.*

ON AUGUST 7, 2007, SAN FRANCISCO GIANTS BASEBALL slugger Barry Bonds was standing at the plate against Washington Nationals pitcher Mike Bacsik. Bonds was awaiting the perfect pitch to make history. It came, and with one violent swing of the bat, Bonds sent a deep fly ball over the right-field fence. As soon as the ball left his bat, he knew. He threw his hands up in celebration and grinned from ear to ear. Home run number 756—a mark that eclipsed the all-time record, previously held by the beloved Hank Aaron. Yes, there were celebrations, but even more so, there were questions.

Four years earlier, Bonds was the centerpiece of the BALCO fiasco, one of the largest performance-enhancing-drug scandals in history. When the FBI raided the BALCO laboratory just outside of San Francisco, agents found an elaborate system of drug use spanning multiple professional sports. In a single raid, the world's fastest man (100-meter-sprint world-record-holder Tim Montgomery) and the emerging home-run king (Bonds) both had their reputations ruined. Fast-forward to 2007: When Bonds broke Aaron's record, he did so against a backdrop of indisputable evidence that he had cheated.*

After Bonds, baseball needed a savior. Someone who could salvage the reputation of the sport and rightfully take from Bonds what he had stolen from Aaron. It seemed the perfect man for the job was a shortstop who entered the league at just eighteen years old and cemented himself as a star by twenty. A man who, by the age of thirty-one, had collected 518 home runs and was well on his way to breaking Bond's tainted record. Everyone in and around the sport loved him. Broadcasters, commentators, fans, and even other players consoled themselves, saying, "Bonds won't have the record for long, A-Rod will get it soon." A-Rod, of course, was the nickname given to Alex

---

* The fact that a convicted cheater could break the sport's most prestigious record was made possible by Major League Baseball, which never had the guts to suspend Bonds.

Rodriguez. And in 2009, as he was closing in on the home-run record, indisputable evidence emerged that led Rodriguez to confess that he, too, had used steroids.

Major League Baseball's drug problem is not surprising. Researchers from the University of Waterloo found that athletes who are obsessively passionate are more likely to engage in doping, or the illicit use of performance-enhancing substances like steroids.[12] In a separate study, when Olympians were asked if they would take a drug that guaranteed them a gold medal but would kill them in five years, half of them said yes.[13]

How could athletes at the top of their game, already making millions of dollars, risk their health, fame, and fortune for seemingly small improvements? The massive risk they're taking compared to the benefits seems absurd. Yet athletes—along with Holmes, Skilling, and countless other professionals—take such irrational risks year after year. They become so obsessed, so focused on and tied to external results, that nothing else matters. It's not that they are no longer passionate. It's just that they are no longer passionate about baseball, or energy, or leading a company, or scientific discovery. They become passionate only about results, fortune, fame, and winning. Upon retirement, Alex Rodriguez was asked for his top three pieces of career advice. Sitting at number one? "Find your passion."[14]

By now, it should be clear that the dark, bad kind of passion rears its ugly head when we become passionate not about an activity but about the external validation and success it might bring. When we become so tied to results it's hard to separate our literal "selves" from the outcome of our passions. Yet this isn't the only way passion can turn into suffering; this also happens when passion gets hijacked by fear. In particular, fear of failure.

PASSION PRACTICES

- Beware of your passion becoming obsessive. This happens when you become less passionate about *doing* an activity than you are about achieving external results and the validation that comes from doing that activity.
- When you are obsessively passionate, your sense of self becomes fused with the external results of your work.
- No amount of success is enough. If you crave external validation, you'll always want more: more money, more fame, more followers. Behavioral scientists call this cycle of endless desire hedonic adaptation. Long before that, the Buddha called this suffering.
- When people who embody obsessive passion fail, experience setbacks, or even just plateau, they often feel completely devastated. As a result, obsessive passion is linked to anxiety, depression, burnout, and unethical behavior.

FUELED BY FEAR

In order to understand the power fear holds over us, it is once again instructive to reflect on our deep past. On the African savanna, as our species was maturing sometime between *Homo erectus* and *Homo sapiens,* fear, and especially fear of failure, served as a critical competitive advantage. Each and every hunt was not only an opportunity to obtain meat for nourishment, but also an opportunity to be maimed by predators and other aggressive beasts. Back then, failure generally meant death. As a result, we evolved to avoid failure with the same innately programmed intensity that we evolved to crave the chase.

Anyone who has ever encountered a bear on a hike, or perhaps even a stranger at night on an empty street, is familiar with the power of fear. Our heart rate soars. Adrenaline floods our veins and courses through our body. Our perceptions heighten. Our world narrows, becoming nothing more than a series of steps to avoid disaster. True, bone-deep fear ignites within us perhaps the most primitive and powerful kind of passion there is: the passion to survive. There's no denying that fear can drive us to accomplish incredible feats. It's why our species is still around today, why the inflammatory basketball coach Bobby Knight's teams won championships, and why tyrant bosses often get impressive results out of their employees (for a time, anyway). But passion that is rooted in fear comes at quite a cost. And rarely, if ever, is it sustainable.

IF THE NAME DOMINIQUE MOCEANU SOUNDS FAMILIAR, that's because it was headlining the national news during the 1996 Summer Olympics in Atlanta, Georgia. The petite fourteen-year-old was part of the "Magnificent Seven," the US Olympic women's gymnastics team that won the country's first-ever team gold medal in the sport. Moceanu was on the cover of magazines, on morning talk shows, and the topic of newspaper headlines across the country. She was America's darling, a peppy teenager with a smile that could light up any room.

> *Passion that is rooted in fear comes at quite a cost. And rarely, if ever, is it sustainable.*

Gymnasts tend to peak early, but certainly not *that* early, at age fourteen. For Moceanu, the 1996 Olympic Games should have marked the beginning of an illustrious career, with her best days ahead of her and the future of US gymnastics in her hands. But four years later, instead of cementing her legacy on the mat at the Sydney Olympics during what should have been her prime, Moceanu was watching the games from her couch at home, depressed, despondent, and burnt out.

No doubt about it, Moceanu was passionate about gymnastics. She practiced at least twenty-five hours a week starting at the age of seven. The bars, the beam, the vault, and the mat were as big a part of her life as anything else. But her drive didn't come from within, at least not fully. Rather, it was fueled by a fear of what her authoritarian parents and coach would do to her if she didn't excel and win. In her heartfelt memoir, *Off Balance*, Moceanu writes:

> The time leading up to the 1996 Olympics was the most demanding and stressful of my career. The sport I had loved so much was slowly becoming a nightmare as I trained with [my coaches] Béla and Márta Károlyi the summer before the Olympics. I pushed myself as hard as I could, but I always felt like I couldn't please them . . . As much as Béla and Márta treated me with disdain and lack of respect, I kept trying to gain their approval. I feared [Coach] Béla like I feared my father, Tata, yet I still tried to please both of them.[15]

Even after winning gold in 1996, when the other six gymnasts on the Magnificent Seven were celebrating, Moceanu was disappointed. "I realized then that no matter how much I wanted to feel happy, my happiness depended on what my coaches and parents thought of my performance and whether or not *they* were pleased with me," she writes. "It was hard to be happy when I felt I wasn't perfect enough for them."[16]

Evidently, Moceanu wasn't competing out of joy and love for the sport of gymnastics, or at least that wasn't the predominant source of her passion. Rather, she was competing to achieve results that would protect her from the wrath of her coaches and parents. Her smile and enthusiastic demeanor? Quite possibly all an act, in service of winning and born out of fear. It wasn't long before the pressure Moceanu felt became toxic, as evidenced by overtraining and injury. Everything came to a head in 1999 when, as a seventeen-year-old, Moceanu asked a US court to grant her emancipation from her parents. The court agreed. The weight of Moceanu's passion—or, more accurately, the weight of her fear—resulted in a promising career, and childhood, cut short.

On one hand, Moceanu's story illustrates how passion, and even elite performance, can be fueled by fear. A recent review of studies on passion found that in individuals who fear failure, just *thinking* about failure can improve their performance.[17] In one study, participants were assessed as to whether or not they feared failure. Next, they squeezed a handgrip as hard as possible. Then, half of them were instructed to reflect on and write about recent failures while the other half was instructed to reflect on and write about recent successes. Following the writing exercise, all participants squeezed the handgrip again. In those who didn't fear failure,

As a long-term motivator, fear of failure quickly becomes toxic.

whether they thought about success or failure had no effect on performance. But in those who did fear failure, thinking and writing about failure resulted in a significant improvement in grip strength. Similar studies found the same pattern held true even when the test of performance wasn't squeezing a handgrip but something more cerebral, like solving word puzzles. "When [participants] are threatened, they are motivated to redeem themselves," says Jocelyn Bélanger, a psychologist at New York University and the paper's lead author. Yet Moceanu's story also highlights another truth about fear-driven passion: how unhealthy and unsustainable it is. "Fear of failure can help if you're starting a new job and have to make your mark," explains Bélanger. "But it can also lead to burnout, increased stress, and decreased longevity."[18] As a long-term motivator, fear of failure quickly becomes toxic.

In another study, David Conroy, a professor at the College of Health and Human Performance at Penn State, specifically examined athletes like Moceanu who were motivated by fear.[19] He discovered five common drivers:

1. Fear of shame and embarrassment.
2. Fear of losing a positive self-image.
3. Fear of an uncertain future.
4. Fear of important others losing interest.
5. Fear of upsetting important others.

Conroy also learned that while each of these fears can be a strong motivator for a short while, none are sustainable.

When we are overcome by fear, we evaluate everything as a threat. Our body and mind prepare us to survive by any means possible. But what is an effective survival response in the short run almost always morphs into anxiety in the long run. We may reach our goal—perhaps an Olympic medal, straight A's, or praise and promotion from our boss—but by the time we do, we are literally exhausted, totally burnt out. Our minds and bodies can only stay on high alert for so long. Not even the most adventurous hiker wants to be perpetually thinking that every rustle of leaves is a bear about to attack.

"When fear dies, you begin to live."

When we shed fear, it's not that we become complacent. If anything, we become even more inclined to push the envelope, take chances, and express our authentic selves. We go from playing "not to lose" to playing to win. In psychology, this is referred to as the difference between a prevention and promotion mind-set. Under a prevention mind-set, we are focused on doing whatever we can to avoid loss—to protect what we have and play it safe. Sometimes a prevention mind-set can be effective, but it often holds us back from fully self-actualizing. Under a promotion mind-set, however, we stop taking the safe route, or the route someone else wants us to take, or the route we *think* someone else wants us to take. Instead, we become willing to take constructive risks because we aren't afraid of failing. In doing so, we open ourselves up to breakthroughs.

Shedding fear requires "having confidence in your knowledge, skills, and resources, as well as a belief in your ability to succeed and a constant hunger for improvement and growth," according to Ashley Merryman, a talent development researcher. Still, Merryman acknowledges that it's hard to go for it, especially as we get closer to our goal, something she calls the "goal looms closer effect," or "when you've come so far that you just don't want to mess up now."

If you start to fall into this trap, feeling hesitation and fear creep in, ask yourself exactly what it is that you fear. If the answer is messing up or losing, remember that the best way to avoid those outcomes is by playing to win.

Psychologist Stan Beecham, who counsels numerous elite athletes and high-ranking executives, also believes that our relationship with fear is utterly critical to what we will accomplish in our lives: "It's all about fear. If you kill fear, you win. If you kill fear, you have your best year ever. If you kill fear, you train like a mad man. If you kill fear, you go to college for free. If you kill fear, you stand on the podium, you get paid, you have strangers walk up to you and call you by name. When fear dies, you begin to live."[20]

PASSION PRACTICES

- Fear can be a powerful short-term motivator, but in the long term, being driven by fear is unsustainable.
- Passions that are fueled by fear quickly become toxic.
- When we shed fear, we go from playing "not to lose" to playing to win. When we play to win, we take constructive risks that often lead to breakthroughs.
- Everyone has fears. Working to overcome them is often the key to sustainable passion, performance, and happiness.

THIS CHAPTER DISCUSSED THE TWO MAIN FORMS THAT the dark, bad kind of passion takes, both of which are detrimental to long-term performance, health, and happiness:

1. The rewards-driven variety, in which an individual becomes addicted to external results, recognition, and the validation of others.

2. The fear-driven variety, in which someone does anything it
    takes to avoid failure, not wanting to disappoint others or
    themselves.

In both cases, passion is fueled by something other than a
joy of the pursuit itself. And in both cases, passion easily turns
into *passio*, suffering.

As we're about to learn, what separates the good, productive, healthy, and sustainable passion from its darker manifestation is very much related to the reason for which you
undertake an activity. And not just what you tell yourself, but
what you actually feel and believe. This isn't to say you should
(or can) completely disregard external results and/or a fear of
failure. Unless you have the perfect genetics, vast mental training, and years of spiritual guidance, doing so isn't possible.
Every athlete gets a jolt from winning. Every writer feels good
when they sell books. Even every Facebook or Twitter user gets
at least a slight tingle upon receiving a new friend, follower, or
"like." And while some of us may not fear failing others, deep
down inside we all fear, even if only a little bit, failing ourselves.
The key is to recognize these emotions when they arise and to
keep them at bay, to prevent them from becoming the predominant forces underlying your passion.

When you sit down to write, you should sit down to write,
not to sell books. When you show up to work, you should show
up to make a meaningful contribution, not to get promoted
or earn bonuses. When you train and compete, you should do
so to get better, to master your body,
not to win awards or improve in the
rankings. When you love—be it a partner or a child—you should do so out of

*Your passion should not come
from the outside. It should come
from within.*

nurturing a special relationship between you and the object of your affection, not because you fear losing them or because you want to chronicle your relationship on social media for all your "friends" to see. In other words, your passion should not come from the outside. It should come from within.

This is harmonious passion, a far more desirable type of passion; the type that you want in your life. Harmonious passion is the best kind of passion. It is associated with enhanced long-term performance, vitality, health, and overall life satisfaction. It emerges when you are present in the moment and pursuing something out of love, not out of external desires or fear. Unfortunately, achieving and maintaining harmonious passion doesn't happen automatically. But with a particular mind-set and some deliberate work, it *is* accessible to anyone.

5

The Best Kind of Passion

n music, harmony occurs when a combination of tones is played simultaneously and in perfect accord. It's a sound that is nearly impossible to describe, yet immediately recognizable. You know it not only because you hear it, but also because you feel it. Everything clicks. There is complete concordance.

Imagine if the same feeling you experience in the presence of musical harmony could be elicited by thinking about or, better yet, engaging in your passion. If you could know on a level far beyond what words can express that your relationship with your passion is just right. That you are doing exactly what you are supposed to be doing and for all the right reasons. If you could feel this in your bones.

Enter harmonious passion: a feeling that emerges when you are wrapped up in something primarily for the joy of the activity, when your engagement is not merely a means to an end but rather an end in itself.* Harmonious passion manifests mainly

---

* The term *harmonious passion* was coined by Robert Vallerand, the psychologist who also named *obsessive passion*. Along with obsessive

from activities that are freely chosen without contingencies; when you do something because you enjoy it, not because it offers potential rewards, and not to avoid negative repercussions. Not every moment of harmonious passion is necessarily pleasing, but overall, it is deeply fulfilling. It aligns closely with the ancient Greek notion of *eudaimonia,* or a kind of happiness that results not from overwhelming pleasure but from striving to meet one's full potential by engaging in activities that one considers meaningful. In the 1970s, the late psychologist and humanist philosopher Erich Fromm wrote of something similar, which he called productive activity, where happiness isn't related to the attainment of possession or rewards but rather to "the process of ever growing aliveness . . . for living as fully as one can is so satisfactory that concern for what one might or might not attain has little chance to develop."[1] The great paradox, however, is that although external achievement is never a primary goal of harmonious passion, when you become completely immersed in what you're doing for the joy of the activity itself, it is often a by-product. Those who focus most on success are least likely to achieve it. Those who focus least on success, and focus on the process of engaging in their craft instead, are most likely to achieve it.

> Those who focus most on success are least likely to achieve it. Those who focus least on success, and focus on the process of engaging in their craft instead, are most likely to achieve it.

Much like a beautiful harmonious sound, harmonious passion doesn't just magically arise. Rather, it requires deliberate work and practice. This is especially true in a culture that tends to overtly encourage the dark side of passion. Our result-

---

passion, harmonious passion is the second part of what Vallerand calls the dualistic model of passion.

oriented, instant-gratification-obsessed culture tempts us to judge ourselves by the social media popularity contest and trains our eye on external achievements and wins. Creating and sustaining harmonious passion—the best kind of passion—demands going against the grain and cultivating a radically different mind-set.

Passion Practices

- Harmonious passion occurs when you become passionate about an activity for the joy you get out of doing the activity itself.
- Harmonious passion is linked to health, happiness, performance, and overall life satisfaction.
- Harmonious passion does not happen automatically. It must be cultivated with deliberate intention.

THE MASTERY MIND-SET

Mastery is a mind-set and also a path. It leads to continual improvement and development. It values acute (in the moment) and chronic (over a lifetime) engagement but devalues most of the transient stuff in between (point-in-time successes or failures). Mastery is not a new-age self-help concept. It is rooted in principles that are central to psychology and biology, and it is an ever-present theme in the lives of people who embody harmonious passion.

Individuals who are on the path of mastery not only

accomplish great things, but do so in a healthy and sustainable manner. They exude a Zen-like aura, are resistant to burnout, and produce work that is of a special kind of quality—a quality that is born out of love. And yet perhaps their greatest accomplishment is an even more cherished one: continual growth and development, a fulfilling life. Just about every great performer who embodies and sustains the best kind of passion also adheres to what we call the mastery mind-set. The good news is that this mind-set and all its benefits are available to anyone who is willing to put in the work necessary to adopt it. The following subsections describe the six individual components of the mastery mind-set and offer insights on how you can bring each to life.

1. Mastery Mind-Set: Drive from Within

Individuals on the path of mastery are driven from within. Their primary motivation isn't external measures of success or fear, and it's certainly not satisfying others or conforming to a certain peer group or social norms. Rather, their motivation originates from an internal desire to improve and engage in an activity for its own sake. Again, this doesn't mean that each day of their pursuit will be exciting or pleasurable. But it does mean that they will show steadfast enthusiasm about the *totality* of their journey.

Take, for example, an Olympic swimmer on the path of mastery. She is unlikely to be enthusiastic about every workout. And while she'll certainly be excited for the Olympic Games, that still won't be her primary motivation. Rather, her focus will be on her overall progression as a swimmer—on pushing her physical and psychological capabilities and evolving her stroke and its relationship with the water. Following races in which she wins gold medals, after all the other competitors have filed out of the arena to celebrate, she'll be alone in the pool working on her stroke, making subtle adjustments—trying to get better even though she's just been crowned the best. If this swimmer sounds like someone you've heard of, that's because, odds are, you have. Her name is Katie Ledecky. She's on the path of mastery, and after winning five gold medals at the recent Rio Olympic Games, she's quickly becoming one of the most decorated female athletes ever. Ledecky reportedly turned down at least $5 million per year in sponsorship money—along with the additional fame that would have accompanied it—so she could swim at the collegiate level at Stanford University. When she was asked if it was a difficult decision, she simply replied, "No. It wasn't."[2] She knew deep down inside that she wanted the experience of swimming collegiately, and she thought doing so would be better for her long-term development.

Individuals on the path of mastery are driven from within.

How similar are you to Katie Ledecky? We're not talking about your swimming prowess or your ability at anything, for that matter. We're talking about your mind-set. From where does your motivation predominantly come? *Predominantly* is key here. Unless you're a robot, there is no avoiding that a part of your drive will stem from external results and trying to avoid failure. Katie Ledecky *wanted* to win all those medals at the Rio Olympic Games, and surely there was some part of her that didn't want to disappoint her coaches, her fans, or herself. But even more than wanting to win gold or meet expectations, Ledecky wanted to progress as a swimmer. Why else would she be practicing *after* dominating in all her events, or turn down millions of dollars to swim for Stanford? The lion's share of her drive comes from within. Ledecky doesn't judge herself against others so much as she judges herself against prior versions of herself and the effort she is exerting in the present moment. This is about as healthy a form of competition as there is.

It's worth repeating: The mastery mind-set acknowledges that external motivators—be it Olympic medals, book sales, art commissions, or venture capital funding—will influence your motivation. At the same time, however, the mastery mind-set ensures that the influence of such external motivators takes a backseat. This doesn't happen unthinkingly. It requires deliberate choices and actions to keep such external motivators from staking too great a claim in your psyche and inconspicuously turning your passion into *passio*. Perhaps the simplest and most effective of these actions is showing up and doing the work, every damn day.

Doing the work has a special way of putting both success and failure in their respective places. After a massive achievement or a devastating failure, getting back to work serves as an embodied reminder that external results aren't why you are in this. You are in this because you love what you do. Because you are pursuing mastery—a commitment to your craft and ongoing progression in it. You aren't so much *striving for specific goals* as you are *being present in an ongoing practice.*

Don't judge yourself against others. Judge yourself against prior versions of yourself and the effort you are exerting in the present moment. This is about as healthy a form of competition as there is.

- Your book hit the *New York Times* bestseller list? Write. Doing so will be humbling and remind you that you prefer writing books to talking about writing books. Your book flopped and failed to sell more than a hundred copies? Write. Doing so will be cathartic and draw you back into your craft.
- Your start-up attracted $1 million in seed funding? Get to

work on executing the plan and start prospecting immediately. Your start-up failed to attract seed funding? Get to
work on refining the plan and seeking other investors.

- You won multiple gold medals in the Olympics? Swim. You
  failed to live up to external expectations in the Olympics?
  Swim.

Sure, it's only human to get a jolt of excitement after a big
win or to feel disappointment after a tough loss. Enjoy the success or grieve the defeat, but within twenty-four hours, return
to your craft, get back to work. Here are two additional examples, both a bit more intimate, of how this plays out:

1. After Brad writes something that receives a positive recep-
   tion from others, right when he starts feeling a bit vain about
   it, he forces himself to start on his next piece of work. Doing
   so has an immediate humbling effect. He uses the same
   strategy when he writes something that tanks. Rather than
   feel sorry for himself, he starts on the next project. By doing this, he is reminded that he loves writing far more than getting recognized for it. It's a tried-and-true means of preventing the emotions associated with external recognition or failure from staking too great a claim on his motivation.

   > Doing the work has a special way of putting both success and failure in their respective places. After a massive achievement or a devastating failure, getting back to work serves as an embodied reminder that external results aren't why you are in this.

2. When coaching an athlete, regardless of the athlete's age,
   Steve has a twenty-four-hour rule: After a competition,
   the athlete has twenty-four hours to celebrate or ruminate
   about his performance. After two days, however, it's back to
   the grind, back to putting in the work required to get better.

After a poor performance, getting back to work silences the negative voice in his head. After a triumphant performance, getting back to work prevents complacency from laying down even a single root.

Big wins and tough losses share at least one thing in common: It is admittedly hard to get back to work after them. Force yourself to overcome this resistance.

In addition to the physical act of getting back to work, another powerful way to maintain drive from within lies in your psyche; in particular, internalizing the mastery mind-set as a core value. Core values are guiding principles that help dictate your behaviors. They serve as unwavering guides, influencing how you think, feel, and act. Core values are not just beliefs you pay lip service to but those that you truly strive to embody. Research shows that reflecting on your core values helps to ensure that you live in accordance with them. For a recent study published in the *Proceedings of the National Academy of Sciences,* researchers from the University of Pennsylvania and the University of Michigan scanned the brains of people who were reflecting deeply on their core values. Sure enough, they found intensified neural activity in a part of the brain associated with "positive valuation." In other words, when you reflect on your core values, you literally change your brain in a productive manner. Perhaps even more meaningful is that these effects weren't just confined to the brain. The study participants who reflected on their core values went on to overcome challenges in real life.[3]

The implications of this research are fairly straightforward. After a great achievement or a harrowing failure, ask yourself if

> *Enjoy the success or grieve the defeat, but within twenty-four hours, return to your craft, get back to work.*

your response—both what you are feeling on the inside and how you express it on the outside—is aligned with a core value of mastery. Doing so prevents the powerful emotions that accompany both success and failure from hijacking the motivational centers of your brain and refocuses you on the mastery mindset. Brief as it may be, this kind of reflection stops emotional inertia—and the obsessive passion it can lead to—in its tracks.

Drive from within does not occur on its own. Without rapidly coming back to your work and committing to mastery as a core value, external motivators are likely to creep into and eventually dominate your psyche. Do not let this happen. In the now classic book *Letters to a Young Poet,* Rainer Maria Rilke compels his young pupil to escape from reliance on external motivators: "You ask whether your verses are good. You ask me. You have asked others before. You send them to magazines. You compare them with other poems, and you are disturbed when certain editors reject your effects . . . I beg you to give up all that. You are looking outward, and that above all you should not do . . . there is only one single way. Go into yourself."[4] Rilke's lesson is clear: Proactively nurture your intrinsic motivation.

IT'S ALSO IMPORTANT TO NOTE THAT MOTIVATIONAL PATterns are finicky and start early in life. If you work with children in any manner, do encourage them to follow their interests and support their natural talents. Do *not* exert too much pressure or emphasize external rewards (for achievement) or punishment (for failure). Your actions will either promote or suppress the mastery mind-set. Far too many parents, teachers, and coaches teach children to measure their value based on external signals or results. This is counterproductive. In the words of Timothy Gallwey, author of the classic book *The Inner*

Game of Tennis, "Children who have been taught to measure themselves in this way often become adults driven by a compulsion to succeed which overshadows all else. The tragedy of this belief is not that they will fail to find the success they seek, but that they will not discover the love or even the self-respect they were led to believe will come with it."[5]

PASSION PRACTICES

- Work to maintain your inner drive, or motivation that comes predominantly from within.
  - Adhere to the twenty-four-hour rule. After failures and successes, give yourself twenty-four hours to feel either sad or happy, then return to your craft. Getting back to work helps put external drivers in their place, behind the importance of internal ones.
  - Internalize drive from within as a core value: When you start to feel yourself getting overly emotional about failures, successes, or external validation, pause and reflect on what you like most about your work. Remind yourself that drive that comes from within is healthier and more sustainable than drive that comes from external sources.
- If you are a parent, coach, manager, or teacher, encourage internal over external motivation in those you lead.

---

2. Mastery Mind-Set: Focus on the Process

At the most recent USA Track & Field Olympic trials in Eugene, Oregon, twenty-eight-year-old Brenda Martinez was in prime position to win her best event, the 800-meter run, which would qualify her for her first Olympics. But with less than one hundred meters to go, a trailing runner tripped and fell forward into Martinez, throwing her off balance. Martinez was able to regain her footing, but not before being passed by a handful of other runners who would secure the three Olympic spots. It was devastating to watch.

Martinez could have felt distraught and dejected. She failed to achieve her goal of making the Olympics in her strongest event, and almost entirely due to bad luck. But Martinez is made of strong stuff. Instead of feeling sorry for herself, immediately following the race she told reporters that she was focused on getting ready for the 1,500-meter run, her secondary event that she had also qualified to compete in. "The track doesn't care about your feelings," she said. "You've just got to move forward." And that's exactly what she did. Less than one week later, in her *sixth* race of the Olympic trials, the 1,500 meters, Martinez literally dove across the finish line to secure third place—by three one-hundredths of a second—earning her opportunity to represent the United States in Rio. What's even more remarkable is that she accomplished this in an event that she wouldn't have even raced in had she not been (literally) thrown off her feet in her primary event.

It's easy to see how Martinez could have lost focus and been sucked into a vicious cycle of rumination. Or worse, how she could have become depressed or burnt out. If any situation was going to trigger the dark side of passion, it was a failure, on the sport's biggest stage, in the 800 meters, which resulted from no fault of her own. But when Brad spoke with Martinez for a *New York* magazine interview shortly after these events unfolded, she told him that it was the same mind-set that got her to the Olympic trials in the first place—after ten years of training that included setbacks, false milestones, and close calls—that got her through it. "I just quickly let go of what happened in the 800 meters and got back to my routine, to focusing on all the little things I could do that would give me the best chance of running well later in the week," she told Brad.[6] Brenda Martinez wasn't a slave to her goal of making the Olympic team. She was focused on the *process.*

We're not sharing Martinez's story to say that you should never set and strive for big goals. Goals are like steering mechanisms, North Stars to shoot for, and when used in this manner they are very productive. But as you've learned by now, too much focus on a specific goal, and especially one that is outside your full control (like winning a race), almost always does more harm than good. The mastery mind-set involves shifting your focus from achieving any one goal itself to executing on the *process* that gives you the best chance of more general improvement over time. Someone who embodies the mastery mind-set judges herself based not on whether she accomplishes her specific goal but rather on how well she executes her process. After all, it is the process, not the outcome, that is within your control.

Focusing on the process also means breaking down goals into their component parts and concentrating on those parts. It's an incredible focusing mechanism that keeps you in the here and now, even during the pursuit of distant goals or in the face of setbacks or failure. For Martinez, this meant not worrying about her bad luck in the 800 meters and instead ensuring she got in the proper nutrition, body-work, sleep, and workouts to give herself the best chance of running a good race in the 1,500 meters. She wasn't overly attached to the external validation that would come from making the Olympics. She was focused on the process of doing the best she could.

Someone who embodies the mastery mind-set judges herself based not on whether she accomplishes her specific goal but rather on how well she executes her process.

This mind-set is integral to maintaining harmonious passion over the long and rocky road to a big event like the Olympics, but it can be applied to just about any passion—from finishing a painting to earning a promotion to improving a relationship. First, set a goal—but remember, it should serve more as a direction than a destination. Next, figure out the steps that are required to make progress toward that goal and that are within your control. Then (mostly) forget about the goal, and focus on nailing the steps instead.

Focusing on the process creates daily opportunities for little victories. These little victories serve as waypoints on the path of mastery, helping to sustain your motivation over the long haul. Numerous studies, including one published in the prestigious science journal *Nature*, provide insight into why this is the case.[7, 8] Researchers have found that when mice accomplish micro objectives on the path to distant goals (e.g., making a correct turn in a maze), their bodies release dopamine, the neurochemical associated with motivation and drive. Without hits of dopamine, the mice become apathetic and give up. Although these studies cannot be safely replicated in humans, scientists speculate we operate the same way. Process spurs progress, and progress, on a deep neurochemical level, primes us to persist.

Perhaps even more important than what it does for your

Focusing on the process creates daily opportunities for little victories. These little victories serve as waypoints on the path of mastery, helping to sustain your motivation over the long haul. Process spurs progress, and progress, on a deep neurochemical level, primes us to persist.

motivation, focusing on the process also ensures that your self-worth never hinges on events that are outside of your control, like getting tripped during an Olympic qualifying event. It keeps the dark side of passion at bay—not allowing too much of your self-worth to rely on the achievement of an external goal. Focusing on the process also fosters a wonderful sense of internal satisfaction that comes with knowing that you put in the work; a special kind of confidence, fullness, and contentment that no one can take away from you. It's a way of saying, "I did everything in my control, so let the chips fall where they may."

The long-term pursuit of a passion will inevitably contain both accomplishments and failures, but you must remember that the path of mastery is never-ending. Focusing on the process helps you stay level-headed, remain poised, and maintain motivation along the way. Don't spend too much time reflecting on whether you achieved specific goals. Spend time reflecting on *how well you adhered to a process* that gives you the best chance of progressing in your chosen pursuit. A goal is a direction, not a destination. Process keeps you present on your journey.

3. Mastery Mind-Set: Don't Worry About Being the Best—Worry About Being the Best at Getting Better

You just learned the importance of not becoming overly attached to specific goals, but becoming attached to the ultimate goal—getting better—is an inherent part of internalizing the

---

PASSION PRACTICES

- Focus on the process, not on results.
- Yes, set goals, but rather than focusing too much on the goal itself, focus on the steps that are within your control to accomplish the goal. Remember that goals should serve as a direction, not a specific all-or-nothing endpoint.
- Celebrate little victories along the way. Doing so will help you sustain motivation in the pursuit of far-off objectives.
- Understand that if you thoroughly embrace the journey, you are more likely to arrive at the destination feeling good, confident, and satisfied.

---

mastery mind-set and living with harmonious passion. When your utmost goal is simply to get better, all failures and successes are temporary because you will forever improve, given more time and more practice. You don't define yourself by any single moment in time; you define yourself by an entire body of work in service of ongoing growth and development. Your pursuit ceases to be something you are aiming for and becomes a part of who you are. Do you write to sell books, or are you a writer? Do you run to win marathons, or are you a runner? Do you paint to sell portraits, or are you a painter?

When you make this shift—your pursuit transitioning from a verb, something you do, to a noun, someone you are—you're more apt to harmoniously hold on to your passions for life. This isn't to say there won't be rough patches, disappointments, and triumphs along the way. But rather than serving as end-points, concrete achievements and failures become more like information—markers of progress and exposures of weakness—that you can use to improve yourself and your process on a longer path.

In an ironic twist, adhering to a goal of "getting better" can be especially powerful when it seems that you are destined to get worse. That's because in the grand scheme of things, "better" is less about objective results and more about the evolution of your relationship with your passion. For many of the most passionate people, getting better is about becoming stronger, kinder, and wiser. "Better" is about how the practice of your passion transforms you as a person. This shift becomes especially important as we age, losing some of our physical and perhaps even cognitive abilities:

> *You don't define yourself by any single moment in time; you define yourself by an entire body of work in service of ongoing growth and development.*

- Someone who in their youth wrote quickly and mainly to sell books will likely quit in old age. But a *writer* will continue to write, bringing new sources of wisdom and insight to his work. He will understand that the only real failure is putting down the pen.
- Someone who in their youth ran exclusively to win races might take up doubles tennis or water aerobics in old age. But a *runner* will continue to pound the pavement. And even though her finishing times may stagnate—and perhaps "run" will even turn into "jog" or "walk"—her relationship with the sport will continue to evolve and grow. No matter how much she slows down, as long as she keeps training, she will be faster than if she quits, and that in and of itself serves as the primary victory.

In short, when your goal is simply to get better, you set yourself up for a lifetime relationship with your passion, which no longer becomes something you do but rather someone you are. It's a relationship that can withstand the gravest failures, the greatest successes, and the passage of time itself. Whatever your passion may be, set aside a moment to take stock of your goals. If they are pointed toward concrete objectives or win-loss outcomes, consider reframing them in the spirit of mastery. The ultimate goal is to get

For many of the most passionate people, getting better is about becoming stronger, kinder, and wiser.

better—stronger, kinder, and wiser—than your past self. If you can maintain that mind-set, given time, you will reach every goal you can imagine, and possibly some you can't.

PASSION PRACTICES

- The ultimate goal is to get better.
- "Better" doesn't just mean improved objective results.
- Focus on continuous improvement over specific point-in-time results; doing so promotes harmonious passion throughout the good times and the bad.
- Be most intent not on winning or losing, but on becoming better—stronger, kinder, and wiser—than your past self.

4. Mastery Mind-Set: Embrace
Acute Failure for Chronic Gains

A well-known principle of physical training is this: If you want a muscle to grow, you must push it beyond its normal bounds, until it is hard, if not impossible, to perform additional repetitions. In exercise science, this is called training to fatigue. Training to fatigue is so effective because muscle fatigue, or, in some cases, failure, serves as a critical signal, telling your body it must grow and adapt in order to withstand future challenges. When you fail, your body learns, on an innate biological level, what it needs to do differently. Failure sets off a cascade of changes that help you evolve so you can meet a greater challenge next time. In other words, your body can't really grow unless it fails. This principle holds true far beyond your muscles.

For a study published in the journal *Frontiers in Psychology*, talent development researchers Dave Collins, Áine MacNamara, and Neil McCarthy examined why some athletes who were world-class in their youth go on to become world-class as adults (what they call "super champions"), while other athletes, once world-class in their youth, end up in second-rate leagues (the heartbreakingly named "almost champions"). The researchers found that the difference between the super champions and almost champions appears to be at least partially driven by how each group responded to adversity.

The greats rose to the challenge and put in persistent effort; the almost-greats lost steam and regressed. Super champions, the researchers write, "were characterized by an almost fanatical reaction to challenge." They viewed challenges in a positive light—as opportunities to grow—and overcame failure thanks to a "never satisfied" attitude. They always wanted to grow more, to see what they were capable of, to find out for themselves what their "best" really meant. Almost champions, on the other hand, blamed setbacks on external causes, became negative, and lost motivation. Although athletes in each group faced comparable challenges, their responses to those challenges were distinct.[9]

These findings support broader psychological research showing that individuals who have faced adversity and faltered in the past are more likely to show persistent effort and succeed in the future. In business, companies are increasingly seeking out individuals who have failed in the past and recruiting them to run high-profile projects. Consider one of Amazon's latest ventures, AmazonFresh, a service that delivers groceries to your door. To run this project, Amazon hired the former executives of Webvan, another grocery-delivery service (and one of the first-ever attempts at this concept), which went bust in 2001. In a letter to shareholders, Amazon's CEO Jeff Bezos wrote that "failure comes part and parcel with innovation."[10]

Super champions are characterized by an almost fanatical reaction to challenge.

You not only learn from failure, but if you accept it as an inherent part of mastery and view it productively, you overcome it and are hardened by it. So much of this depends on how you internalize failure. Do you attribute failure to variables that you can change, or perhaps just to a dose of downright bad luck that doesn't have much to do with you? Or do you attribute failure to yourself—that you're just not and won't ever be good enough? Far too often, we default to the latter, which leads to a fear of failure that pushes us away from engaging in challenging experiences altogether. This is an acquired trait that begins early on in our youth. Studies show that students who fear failure shut down and quit whatever it is they were working on when the going gets tough.[11] Students who embody more of a mastery orientation, however, continue to forge ahead, looking for alternative solutions.

Shedding your fear of failure starts with working to disconnect your sense of self and ego from the external product of your work. Otherwise, failure becomes an attack on your actual "self," on you as a person. And then you'll go into defensive mode—blaming others, no longer taking chances, or, worse yet, cheating. This is how the dark side of passion took control of some of the high-profile business people and athletes that we briefly profiled in the prior chapter. On the other hand, if you remove your ego from the equation, failure can be a source of rich information and an opportunity to grow. Much like extrinsic motivation, ego can, and often does, subtly creep into the equation. That's why it's important to practice all the elements of the mastery mind-set, which work in tandem to keep ego at bay.

Shedding your fear of failure doesn't mean you should actively seek out failure. But it does free you to pursue bold challenges, to push the envelope. When you do, one of two things will happen: You'll either break through, or you'll fail. Both outcomes are integral to ongoing advancement down mastery's path. No one becomes a master after a single, perfect attempt. Mastery is the product of many failures, each serving an important lesson. If you think of your goal as a direction, not a destination, then failure should be embraced. Each failure provides you more of the knowledge you'll need to continuously get better. What feels like failure in the short term is often essential to making long-term gains. There's an old Eastern proverb that says, "The master has failed more times than the student has even tried." We'd all be wise to take it to heart.

PASSION PRACTICES

- Adopt the mind-set of a super champion.
  - Don't become overly discouraged or saddened by failure.
  - Rather, view failure productively, as something that serves as critical information, as a microscope into areas in which you can improve.
- Remember that what feels like failure in the short term is often essential to your ability to make long-term gains.

---

5. Mastery Mind-Set: Patience

A few simple truths:

- The path of mastery is almost always very hard and requires lots of time and unyielding commitment.
- Any long-term progression contains inevitable periods of boredom.
- We are hardwired to seek novelty and stimulation, which is why "quick fixes" and "hacks" can be so appealing—even though they rarely, if ever, work.
- Advancing on the path of mastery, getting the most out of yourself and sustaining passion for a lifetime, requires patience.

Yet patience is not a given. It is a trait that is becoming exceedingly rare in today's world. If anything, we should probably start treating patience as a valuable skill, a competitive advantage. That's because even though we may not always realize it, modern technology is conditioning us to be less patient and instead expect immediate gratification: what we want, exactly when we want it. Instantaneously and without effort, we can answer an obscure question (Google), chat with someone across the world (Skype), and even land a date (Tinder). While this sort of technology can be wonderful in its ability to shrink the world, a significant downfall is that it also shrinks our attention spans. As a result, we are becoming less comfortable than ever with stillness, with time and space in which seemingly nothing is happening. One recent study showed that people would rather shock themselves electrically than sit alone without a mobile device for even just a few minutes.[12]

Our waning patience is a problem because, in the words of the late author and aikido master George Leonard, "To learn anything significant, to make any lasting change in yourself, you must be willing to spend *most* of your time on the plateau."[13] A willingness to spend time on the plateau is intimately related to the difference between harmonious passion and the dark side of passion. Long before the psychologist Robert Vallerand came up with the term *obsessive passion*, Leonard wrote about what he called the obsessive personality: someone who lacks the patience and stick-to-itiveness required for mastery:

> The Obsessive is a bottom-line type of person, not one to settle for second best. He or she knows results are what count, and it doesn't matter how you get them, just so you get them fast. In fact, he wants to get the stroke right during the very first lesson. He stays after class talking to the instructor. He asks what books and tapes he can buy to help him make progress faster.
>
> The Obsessive starts out by making robust progress. His first spurt is just what he expected. But when he inevitably

regresses and finds himself on a plateau, he simply won't take it. He redoubles his effort. He pushes himself unmercifully. He refuses to accept his boss's and colleagues' counsel of moderation. He works all night at the office, he's tempted to take shortcuts for the sake of quick results.

The Obsessive lives for the upward surge, the swelling background music, the trip to the stars. When ardor cools, he doesn't look elsewhere. He tries to keep the starship going by every means at his command. He doesn't understand the necessity for periods of development on the plateau . . . Somehow, in whatever he is doing, the Obsessive manages for a while to keep making brief spurts of upward progress, followed by sharp declines—a jagged ride toward a sure fall. When the fall occurs, the Obsessive is likely to get hurt. And so are his friends, colleagues, stockholders, and lovers.[14, 15]

The similarities between Vallerand's obsessive passion and Leonard's obsessive personality are striking. All the previously discussed elements of the mastery mind-set—maintaining drive from within, focusing on the process over results, not worrying about being the best but striving to be the best at getting better, and embracing acute failure for chronic gains—require patience. Patience is a first principle, an enabling factor of the

> *"To learn anything significant, to make any lasting change in yourself, you must be willing to spend most of your time on the plateau."*

mastery mind-set and the harmonious passion it yields. Without patience, what starts as harmonious passion can easily turn into obsessive passion, becoming maladaptive and causing harm, pain, and suffering.

It's easy to say that the moral of the story is to have patience and stick with something. But that doesn't mean it is easy to do.

Like we discussed earlier, patience is not an innate trait; it's a skill to be developed. Brett Bartholomew is someone who has experience developing it. He is a renowned strength and conditioning coach to many of the world's best athletes, from NFL all-stars to UFC champions. Almost everyone he works with is immensely passionate; otherwise, they wouldn't be near the top. Bartholomew's challenge is this: Because the athletes he trains are already world-class, making them even better is especially difficult. Even the smallest marginal gains are hard to come by. The last few percentage points of performance—the gaps between good, great, and best-ever—take a long time to close.

When Bartholomew senses an athlete's persistence and discipline are waning—something that is particularly dangerous in sports given the availability of illegal steroids as well as the many ways reckless training can cause injury—he encourages them to reflect on their purpose. This is a great approach, and one we recommend everyone use. It's quick and easy to do: Just ask yourself why you're committed to your pursuit. The importance of reflecting on your purpose is also backed by science. Similar to reflecting on your core values, when you reflect on your purpose, not only do you reinforce the mastery mind-set, but you also become more likely to stick with challenges over the long haul. Of course, if you ask yourself why you are passionate about something and your answer is related to external validation or failure avoidance, it should prompt some serious reflection. But if your answer is aligned with mastery—for example, you're engaged in something to grow, learn, and become a better human being—then regularly coming back to your purpose is a powerful way to remind yourself of the value of staying the course, especially during times of boredom, when you're on the plateau.

In addition to providing a boost in motivation, reflecting on your purpose is beneficial because doing so creates space between impulse—the urge to get upset with every acute failure and take shortcuts or quit—and action. It is within this space that you can remind yourself that there is much about a years-long marriage—be it to a sport, a sculpture, an idea, or a person—that is better than succumbing to the latest and greatest temptation.

Passion Practices

- Patience is not just a virtue; it is a skill that must be developed over time.
- Patience is critical to mastery and harmonious passion. The ability to stay the course and ride out valleys and plateaus separates good from great and harmonious from obsessive passion.
- One of the best ways to remain patient is to reflect on your purpose, or the overarching "why" that underlies your activity. Doing so reminds you why you're in this (whatever your respective "this" may be) in the first place, and also creates some space between impulse and action.

---

6. Mastery Mind-Set: Be Here Now

Step outside and stare at the closest brick wall, or perhaps, as the saying goes, "watch paint dry." Few would find such activities interesting or engaging. If anything, utter boredom would likely ensue. But the philosopher and author Robert Pirsig felt differently. In his classic book *Zen and the Art of Motorcycle Maintenance,* Pirsig makes a case for the power of full engagement in *anything,* even activities that most would consider mind-numbing. He makes his case by relaying a story of a college student he once taught: At first, the student was given an assignment to write an essay about the United States. When she came to class in despair over her inability to formulate an essay, Pirsig suggested she narrow the subject matter down to the city in which they lived—Bozeman, Montana. Still, the student had no luck, coming to class over the next few weeks completely blocked. Pirsig told her the problem was that she wasn't looking hard enough, she wasn't paying close enough attention. "You're not looking! Narrow it down to the front of *one* building on the main street of Bozeman," Pirsig told her. "The Opera House. Start with the upper left-hand brick."

Pirsig describes how the student left class and parked herself in front of the Opera House, where she began staring at the upper left-hand brick. To her astonishment, the words began to flow. Soon enough, she had written not five hundred words, as the original assignment dictated, but five thousand words, all spurred by paying attention to the bricks of the Opera House. Here's Pirsig: "She couldn't think of anything to write about Bozeman because she couldn't recall anything she had heard worth repeating. She was strangely unaware that she could look and see freshly for herself, as she wrote, without primary regard for what had been said before. The narrowing down to one brick destroyed the blockage because it was so obvious she *had* to do some original and direct seeing."[16] For Pirsig, being intimately engaged is the key to seeing things clearly and getting the most out of life.

When we are fully present for whatever it is we are doing, we gain a new appreciation for our respective pursuits and our own unique role in them. Yet the majority of the time, we walk around on autopilot, not deliberately choosing where or how sharply we direct our attention. To sustain passion, however, we must remove distractions that prey on our attention and break from the mundane and automatic thoughts that normally fill our minds. Practically, this means we should set aside the time, space, and energy to give our respective passions our all. It doesn't need to be all day, every day, but we do need to prioritize this time and make it sacred.

Pirsig isn't alone in his belief that even staring at a single brick can be engaging if enough attention is given to it. Other philosophers have said much the same: The motorcycle mechanic and author Matthew Crawford believes that "[t]o take pleasure in an activity is to engage in that activity while being absorbed in it, where this absorption consists in single-minded and lively attention to whatever it is that seems to make the activity good or worth pursuing."[17] The philosopher and writer Alain de Botton puts it like this: "Everything is potentially a fertile subject for art and we can make discoveries as valuable in an advertisement for soap as in Pascal's *Pensées*."[18] Engagement is the secret.

Deep-focused engagement is fuel for harmonious passion. It seems simple and obvious, yet step back and think about just how little receives your full attention. Even activities that once forced us to be present—such as a walk or run in the woods, holding a newborn baby, or a physician's encounter with a patient—are now frequently hijacked by the beeping and buzzing of our digital devices. These modern inventions continuously pull our attention to the next external diversion, creating the illusion that we are both busy and present, all the while keeping us on autopilot and at the whim of whatever distracts us next. Way too often, we may appear to be *here,* but we are really *there.*

Being fully present isn't just the stuff of philosophers and their (at times) esoteric metaphysics. Scientific research demonstrates that how we assign our attention has an enormous influence on what we do from day to day, year to year, and even over the course of a lifetime.[19] According to researchers from Radboud University in the Netherlands, "One of the most important roles for attention is to translate goals into overt behavior."[20] In other words, whatever we channel our attention toward receives a declaration of value, a reinforcing signal that our chosen pursuit is important. And what we deem important is what gets done. It's a bit paradoxical, but the key message here is, what is important doesn't necessarily get our attention; *what gets our attention becomes important.* This explains why so many of us neglect work we believe is "important" and instead spend so much time engaging in other, seemingly trivial distractions. Whatever attracts our attention is king.

Individuals who possess the mastery mind-set understand the importance of attention. Though everyone is distracted occasionally, the mastery mind-set demands that you deliberately carve out time and energy to give the pursuits you value the full attention they deserve. It's only by repeatedly sending a clear message that your pursuit is supremely important—a message that is sent via where you direct your attention—that you gain the discipline and capacity required to resist all the distractions, the "attention vampires," that constantly surround you. If time

> *It's a bit paradoxical, but the key message here is, what is important doesn't necessarily get our attention; what gets our attention becomes important.*

is the most precious resource there is, then attention—or how you spend time—is inherently a part of using it well. When engaging in your passion, be here now.

PASSION PRACTICES

- When you engage in your passion, be intentional about removing distractions so that you can pay full attention.
- Carve out time, space, and energy for periods of single-minded focus.
- Remember: What is important doesn't necessarily get your attention; what gets your attention becomes important. Be intentional about where you direct yours.

In summary, the mastery mind-set contains six key principles:

1. **Driven from within.**
2. **Focus on the process.**
3. **Don't worry about being the best; worry about being the best at getting better.**
4. **Embrace acute failure for chronic gains.**
5. **Be patient.**
6. **Be here now.**

Working to live in alignment with these principles keeps the dark kind of passion at bay and gives rise to harmonious passion, the best kind of passion. And living with the best kind of passion can be a beautiful thing.

LIVING WITH HARMONIOUS PASSION

The philosopher and author Robert Pirsig, whom you met a few pages back, writes about quality not as an adjective, but rather as an event. He describes it as something that occurs when an actor and his or her act are so seamlessly interwoven that they are hard to separate—they become one. Pirsig's Quality (he wrote it with a capital "Q" to represent its singular nature) represents a connection born out of the utmost respect, attention, and caring. It's when an artist working on a sculpture is no longer separate from the marble but becomes a part of it as he shapes it. Or when an athlete becomes so fully rapt in her sport that she is no longer "playing" it but simply flowing as one with it. Or when two lovers know exactly what the other is feeling without saying a word. Pirsig believes that it is during connections like these, connections that embody Quality, that a life is fully lived.[21]

In order to experience Quality, you can't be thinking about the past or the future or what other people may think of you or your work. Rather, you must be completely involved in whatever it is you are doing. Totally there. Fully present. Only by shedding fear and attachment to external results and in turn pursuing something primarily for its own sake does Pirsig's Quality become attainable. Harmonious passion is a conduit to Quality.

Many other great thinkers have taken note of this phenomenon. George Leonard writes that the space between an actor who is dedicated to his act and his act itself is the space in which God lives.[22] Erich Fromm refers to it as a special kind of joy, "what we experience *in the process* of growing nearer [to] becoming one's [authentic] self."[23] When the late scholar Avedis Donabedian, one of the founding fathers of the quality-improvement movement in health-care, was on his deathbed, he was asked how, after all these years, he defines quality. His response: "Quality is love."[24]

In order to experience Quality, you can't be thinking about the past or the future or what other people may think of you or your work. Rather, you must be completely involved in whatever it is you are doing. Totally there. Fully present.

Harmonious passion and the Quality it births are a gateway to a very special experience. It's an experience that elevates not only your work, but also your life. A comprehensive review of the academic literature spanning a variety of domains including art, athletics, and business found that harmonious passion is related to enhanced vitality, emotional engagement, learning, practice, performance, and overall life satisfaction.[25] Put differently, it seems that adopting the mastery mind-set and nurturing the harmonious passion it spawns are the keys to getting the most out of yourself, and the most out of life.

And yet that's still not the whole story. Because even if you embody the mastery mind-set and experience the harmonious passion it brings, really going for something carries an incontestable cost: everything else that you leave behind as a result. Fully throwing yourself into a passion—even if it's the best kind of passion, however harmonious it may be—tends to throw your life out

Harmonious passion and the Quality it births are a gateway to a very special experience. It's an experience that elevates not only your work, but also your life.

of balance. Which begs the question: Is it possible to live a passionate and "balanced" life at the same time? Should you even be striving to in the first place?

Passion Practices

- Adopting the mastery mind-set gives rise to harmonious passion, the best kind of passion, and a special sort of *Quality*: when you become so wrapped up in your activity that you're hard to separate from it—you become one with it.
- In the midst of living with harmonious passion, we often feel more alive than ever.
- Harmonious passion comes with many benefits, such as enhanced vitality, performance, and life satisfaction.
- And yet there is still a cost of living with harmonious passion: everything else that you leave behind when you give your all to something.

6

The Illusion of Balance

Perhaps more than anything, the late world-renowned motivational speaker Jim Rohn championed balance. His words are found on posters lining classrooms, workplaces, and yoga studios around the world. "Life without balance can cost you your health. Life without balance can cost you your spirituality. Life without balance can cost you your wealth and your happiness. So find things to motivate you from all areas of life. Your success depends on it."[1] Rohn's message is a strong one, and one that is certainly not unique to him. Thousands of self-help books include a similar refrain. You might even find a "balance" aisle in your local bookstore. Achieving balance is a foundational tenet of the entire self-help industry.

It's not just motivational speakers and self-help gurus who preach the doctrine of balance. Established universities are in on the game, too. Take, for example, the following sessions from a 2016 course on "optimizing balance" offered at George Washington University in Washington, DC.[2]

- **Analyze Your Life Balance,** which helps students "overcome the internal and external obstacles to achieving balance."
- **Maintaining Balance in Your Life,** in which students learn "techniques that can be used to achieve and preserve balance."
- **Strategies for Better Balance,** which "focuses on the actions [students] can take to achieve a more balanced life."

Though it may seem like balance is currently having its moment, our fascination with it is anything but new. The concept is deeply ingrained in our collective psyche, tracing its roots all the way back to ancient Greece. In 300 BC, Aristotle instructed his followers to strive for the golden mean, or the desirable middle between two extremes, one of excess and the other of deficiency. Around the same time, Plato popularized a "tripartite theory of soul," which revolved around keeping the different parts of one's soul in alignment. One of the earliest principles of medicine held that we contain four humors (yellow bile, black bile, phlegm, and blood), which, when a person is healthy, are in perfect balance. Disease, the thinking went, occurred when any one of these humors was in excess or deficit. In art, Leonardo da Vinci's *Vitruvian Man* represented an idealized human body as a perfectly symmetrical one, a balanced one. Throughout history and across diverse contexts, we have always sought balance.

Against that backdrop, it's not at all surprising that today's prevailing wisdom glorifies balance. If only we could find balance, everything else would be all right. Balance. Balance. Balance. But then again, have you ever met an interesting person—let alone a deeply passionate one—who is balanced? Think about your own experiences. During the times when you've felt most alive, have you also felt balanced? For us personally, the answer is a resounding no. Whether it's falling in love, trekking in the Himalayas, writing a book, or training to go as fast as we can in a sport, during these bouts of full-on living, we were completely *consumed* by our activities. Trying to be balanced—devoting equal portions of time and energy to other areas of our lives—would have detracted from the formative experiences. And in this sentiment, we are not alone.

Nearly all the great performers—from athletes to artists to computer programmers to entrepreneurs—whom we've gotten to know through our coaching, reporting, and writing can draw a direct line between being happy, fulfilled, and at their best and going all in on something. Rich Roll, the top ultra-endurance athlete whom you met in chapter 2, told us that "the path to fulfillment in life, to emotional satisfaction, is to find what really excites you and channel your all into it." Dr. Michael Joyner, a groundbreaking researcher at the Mayo Clinic, says,

Have you ever met an interesting person—let alone a deeply passionate one—who is balanced?

"You've got to be a minimalist to be a maximalist; if you want to be really good, master and thoroughly enjoy one thing, you've got to say no to many others." Nic Lamb, one of the best big-wave surfers on the planet, speaking of his relentless pursuit of excellence in the water, puts it like this: "The best way to find contentment is to give something your all."[3]

PASSION AND BALANCE ARE ANTITHETICAL

Before one of us (Steve) became a running prodigy, racing the mile in just over four minutes, his high school coach, a serious and deeply caring man named Gerald Stewart, sat his team down for a pre-season pep talk. Prior to this point, Klein Oak

High School's cross-country team was nothing to be feared. In the school's brief twenty-year history, Klein Oak had never qualified for the State Championship meet. The men's cross-country team at Klein Oak was just like any other cross-country team: an overlooked group of twelve skinny boys who excelled at math and science but, truth be told, struggled at running. Just three years later, however, the school would boast one of the best running programs in not just the state of Texas but the entire country. This swift transformation was due in no small part to the words that made up Stewart's now memorable pre-season pep talk, and his ability to convince a group of twelve teenage boys to live by them.

"Boys, you have a choice," Stewart said. "You can choose to pursue excellence, to be great at something, or you can settle. Most of your peers will choose the latter, choosing the road toward mediocrity, and others will attempt to drag you down, to get you to enjoy the aimless wandering that most do in high school. Some of your friends may be more well-rounded than you, having filled their résumé with various honor societies, debate clubs, student councils, and perhaps an internship or two; but they will never be great. It's my belief that you can only be great at two things at a time. Any more than that and they all suffer. Being on this team and choosing to be great means that your decision has been made: Your two things will be running and school." Coach Stewart knew that his capacity to transform the school's lackluster running program into a formidable force required igniting an intense passion within his runners. He also knew that passion and balance are hard, if not impossible, to reconcile.

Balance implies equilibrium. That you can juggle all the components of life in equal accord. That you can simultaneously be present in all your pursuits. That you can be the best husband, the best father, the best employee, the best student, the best athlete, and so on—and do all these things at once. But this is an illusion, and one that is easily debunked by even just a brief examination of the passionate individual. When someone is wrapped in passion, she is anything but balanced. She is consumed, fully present with and singularly focused on the object of her desire. Ask anyone who has ever really gone for something—who has truly tried to become the best they could be, if not the best, period—and she will tell you that it becomes easy to forget that anything outside her passion exists. Passion is disruptive. Even if it's of the harmonious variety, and even if you develop it incrementally, passion throws your life *out* of balance. Living with passion can be, as one of its original meanings implied, a struggle.

Consider Warren Buffett, one of history's most successful investors. Although Buffett has a net worth of over $75 billion, he lives (and always has lived) a relatively modest life. He only replaces his car, generally a mid-range sedan, once every ten years, and on most days he enjoys a McDonald's breakfast. While the man could live literally anywhere in the world, he makes his home in Omaha, Nebraska, the same modest town in which he was born some eighty-eight years ago. Even when he was younger, Buffett stayed out of the limelight, almost always opting to read voraciously or engage in research rather than attend high-society events. It is ironic that although he is king in the business of money, he seems not to care much at all about the validation that comes from being rich. Buffett simply has no interest in the rat race. His motives are different; they lie purely in wanting to

Passion and balance are hard, if not impossible, to reconcile.

be the best investor he can be. Buffett treats investing as an end in and of itself, as a craft. He embodies the mastery mind-set. As a result, he's become a master.

One thing Buffett is not, however, is balanced. Since he was a child, Buffett has been enthralled by the challenge of investing. When Buffett was in grade school, rather than pursuing normal childhood activities—like sports, girls, and play—he instead spent his time founding and operating a door-to-door delivery service that sold chewing gum, Coca-Cola, and weekly publications. As he grew older, his businesses and investments became more sophisticated and he moved on to detailing automobiles, selling golf balls and stamps, and even purchasing pinball machines to rent out to local barbershops. The comment by his high school yearbook photo simply read: "likes math: a future stockbroker."[4]

Over time, his passion for investing only grew more fervent. Remember, this was not because he wanted to impress others or live a ritzy life—the man's personal strategy is frugality. Buffett became captivated by investing because he loved the challenge of amassing wealth for its own sake. He spent all his time either thinking about financial strategy, evaluating potential investments, or helping companies that he bought improve. And while he did marry and have three children, he was challenged to be fully present for his family. His late wife, Susan, once said, "Physical proximity with Warren doesn't always mean he's there with you."[5]

In the documentary *Becoming Warren Buffett*, his son Howard says that it can be difficult to connect with his father on an emotional level "because that's not his basic mode of operation." Susie, his daughter, says you have to speak to him in short, quick chunks, because "if you went on for too long you would lose him to whatever giant thought he has in his head at the time."[6] Everything on record about Buffett's personal life makes clear that, on one hand, he was well-intentioned and tried to be a real family man. On the other hand, however, it's clear that he was, and still is, fully consumed by investing. Try as he might, he struggles to turn it off. His passion for investing may be harmonious, but it still comes with a cost—in this case, its full-time claim on his attention. In the words of *New Yorker* writer James Surowiecki, "Buffett was born to be great at investing. He had to work really hard to be good at living."[7]

Buffett has plenty of company among passionate individuals, many of whom we celebrate as heroes. Consider two of history's greatest activists, Alexander Hamilton and Mohandas Gandhi. Both men embodied harmonious passion, driven not by ego but by inner motivation and an unwavering belief in something beyond themselves. And yet both had what most would consider flawed personal lives. Hamilton played an integral role in creating the American system of government. At the same time, he engaged in an extramarital affair. Gandhi successfully led India to independence and inspired nonviolent movements for civil rights across the world. For his efforts, he was not only given the name Mahatma, which in Sanskrit means "high-souled," but also the lesser-known Bapu, which is the Hindi word for "father." There is a hefty dose of irony in this: While Gandhi was a father to all of India, he struggled to be a father to his eldest son, Harilal. Their relationship was so troubled that it culminated with Gandhi disowning Harilal.[8]

We can't be sure of the exact reasons why Hamilton's and Gandhi's familial lives suffered. We can only speculate that these men gave so much of themselves to their respective passions for civil rights that they had little left to give to anyone or anything else. These are extreme examples but they highlight a fundamental truth: Our time, attention, and energy are limited. The more passionate we become about any one pursuit, the less of ourselves we have to offer to everything else. This is not necessarily "good" or "bad." It just *is*. Few would wish that Hamilton or Gandhi devoted less of themselves to their causes. And it's damn near impossible to say they lived anything but meaningful lives of productive passion. But their lives certainly weren't balanced.

Buffett, Gandhi, and Hamilton aren't alone. Try to find an Olympic athlete who is balanced. Or a trauma surgeon. Or an award-winning novelist. Or a teenager falling in love for the first time. Or a new parent. Odds are, you'll have a hard time. You simply cannot be deeply passionate and balanced in combination. The roots of passion—both biological and psychological—prevent it. Remember from chapter 2 of this book that passion and addiction are close cousins.

Our time, attention, and energy are limited. The more passionate we become about any one pursuit, the less of ourselves we have to offer to everything else.

Although society deems one productive and the other destructive, both feed off the same underlying drivers and thus tend to become increasingly all-consuming. Living with passion is, by definition, living without balance.

This is a timeless realization, a fact of life that Aristotle understood centuries ago. In his *Nicomachean Ethics*, he wrote, "For people who are fond of playing the flute are incapable of attending to arguments if they overhear someone playing the flute, since they enjoy flute-playing more than the activity in hand; the pleasure connected with flute-playing destroys the activity concerned with argument. This happens, similarly, in all other cases, when one is active about two things at once . . . *This is why when we enjoy anything very much we do not throw ourselves into anything else.*"[9]

The problem isn't that you sacrifice a lot for passion, but

that it's all too easy to let the inertia of a passionate experience carry you forward *without ever really evaluating what you're sacrificing*—for example, time with friends and family, other hobbies, even simple pleasures like catching up on the latest episode of your favorite television show. As you'll see in just a few pages, there's a

Living with passion is, by definition, living without balance.

way to pierce through this inertia and see clearly what really matters in your life and how this can change over time. But before we get to that, we'd be remiss not to address another big risk of living an unchecked passionate life: burnout.

AVOIDING BURNOUT WHILE GOING ALL IN

Lots of people equate a passionate pursuit, going "all in," with working all the time. But this isn't a recipe for sustainable success. It's a recipe for burnout.

As we detailed in our last book, *Peak Performance*, if you want to make lasting progress, you've got to rest. Working hard toward something, or what we call productive stress, doesn't yield growth. Growth only occurs when stress is followed by rest. Or, as the most popular phrase from our last book says, "stress + rest = growth."

It's well established that intrinsic motivation promotes long-term performance and protects against burnout. As we wrote earlier, whether it's on the playing field or in the workplace, the more your drive comes from within and the more you perceive your work as an end in and of itself—that is, you enjoy what you're doing, not just the external rewards and recognition your work brings—the better off you'll be. But that doesn't mean intrinsic motivation makes you bulletproof. Even if you love your work—or perhaps *because* you love your work—if you push too hard without appropriate rest and recovery, you're bound to stagnate.

One of our favorite parts about both of our respective coaching practices is that we get to work with intrinsically motivated and intensely driven people. We rarely, if ever, have to push them forward. That's not the hard part. The hard part is holding them back. Without us putting on the brakes, the athletes, executives, and entrepreneurs we coach would work themselves into the ground—and not in spite of their intrinsic motivation, but because of it. If you are into what you're doing and you're dying to get better, the natural inclination is to keep pushing. Unfortunately, even if that pushing is born of all the right internal reasons, eventually the mind and body get tired. And when the mind and body get tired, it's easy to slip into apathy and, even worse, depression. The worst part of all is that this often happens subtly, without you even realizing it.

And this is to say nothing of the massive importance of sleep. If you really love your work and want to do a good job at it, the *last* thing you should do is sacrifice sleep. In the early 2000s, then groundbreaking research out of Harvard University found that it is during sleep that you retain, consolidate, store, and connect information. In other words, your mind doesn't grow and make leaps when you are at work, but rather when you are at rest.

Even so, it can be excruciatingly hard to step away from your work, especially if you love it. Ernest Hemingway said that as difficult as writing could be, it was "the wait until the next day," when he forced himself to rest, that was his greatest challenge. In his memoir, *On Writing*, Stephen King writes, "For me, not working is the real work."

Inherent in King's quote is a pearl of wisdom. If you consider not working a part of the work, you're more likely to not work. This sentiment is common among the world's best—and *most lasting*—musicians, athletes, artists, intellectuals, executives, and entrepreneurs. They all tend to consider rest an essential part of their jobs. They think about rest *not* as something passive (i.e., nothing is happening, you're wasting time) but rather as something active (i.e., your brain—or, if you're an athlete, your body—is growing and getting better), and thus they're far more liable to respect it. Seen in this light, rest isn't separate from the work—rest is an integral part of the work. Going all in on something doesn't mean you shouldn't rest. If anything, exerting passionate effort is all the more reason to rest. Remember that stress + *rest* = growth. And be sure to build in regular periods of rest and recovery to whatever you do.*

IT'S NOT ABOUT BALANCE—IT'S ABOUT SELF-AWARENESS

In addition to the risk of completely neglecting other important parts of your life (and having regrets later) and burning out, there are also risks inherent to having your identity tied up in a single activity—mainly, what happens when doing that activity is no longer an option? It's not surprising that athletes and super-driven professionals often struggle with depression and other mental health issues when they are forced to retire. It's as if the more you put in, the harder it is to get out. But even so, we don't think that balance—which essentially asks you to never go

---

* For more on rest, see our first book, *Peak Performance: Elevate Your Game, Avoid Burnout, and Thrive with the New Science of Success.* In that book, we devote over sixty pages to "stress + rest = growth" and detail how to apply this equation to diverse pursuits.

all in on anything—is the right solution. Far better than striving for balance is striving for self-awareness, or the ability to see yourself clearly by assessing, monitoring, and proactively managing your core values, emotions, passions, behaviors, and impact on others. Put differently, self-awareness is about creating the time and space to know yourself, constantly checking in with yourself (since your "self" changes over time), and then living your life accordingly.

Someone with keen self-awareness is able to separate the acute euphoria of being fully immersed in a pursuit from the long-term consequences of doing so. It's the Olympian who chooses to retire in time to start and raise a family; the artist who realizes that setting aside some time for life outside the studio gives rise to great works inside the studio; or the lawyer who sets a hard rule of not missing family dinners or her children's sporting events. This type of self-awareness doesn't come easily. Paradoxically, as you're about to learn in the next chapter, one of the best ways to accomplish it is to mentally step outside your "self." Psychologists call this self-distancing, and examples (that you'll soon learn about) include pretending you're giving advice to a friend, journaling in the third person (and then examining the emotions that arise when you read what you wrote), meditating and reflecting on your own mortality.

Practicing self-awareness allows you to more honestly evaluate and reevaluate the trade-offs inherent to living an unbalanced, passionate life. It ensures that you are taking the time to rest and recover so that you don't burn out, and it also ensures that you are making conscious decisions about how you spend your time and energy, and thus decreases the chances that you'll have regrets about what you did—and didn't—do. It helps you realize when your identity may be getting too interwoven with a specific activity, and that in some instances—writing a book, the first few months with a newborn baby, or trying to make an Olympic team, for example—your lack of balance may be excessive, but it can be OK because it's time-bound. For some people, when you zoom in on any given day, week, month, or maybe even year, they don't appear at all balanced. But when you zoom out and look across the totality of their lives, they are actually quite balanced and whole. This is the kind of balance to strive for.

Shalane Flanagan is a thirty-seven-year-old marathon runner who recently became the first American woman to win the New York City Marathon in forty years. Flanagan is deeply passionate about running. When she is in peak training, she regularly logs over 120 miles of running per *week*. She acknowledges and understands that there's simply no way she can be balanced, nor does she want to be. "I like to go all in on one extreme for a period of time and then shift to another extreme," she recently told Brad during an interview for *Outside* magazine. "For me, this means going all in on running, and then taking a vacation where I go all in on things like family and other pursuits. It's too hard—physically and mentally—to try to do everything at once."[10]

Practicing self-awareness allows you to more honestly evaluate and reevaluate the trade-offs inherent to living an unbalanced, passionate life.

Flanagan also realizes that her career as a professional runner is time-bound. There will come a moment when she'll want to, or her body will force her to, point her passion in other directions. Even in the midst of her intense running schedule, she hasn't completely neglected her other interests, like cooking and writing (she recently combined those interests and co-authored a cookbook, *Run Fast. Eat Slow*, with Elyse Kopecky).

Flanagan is also a staple in the running community, so perhaps formal mentoring or even coaching will be in her future. "I want to explore my limits in running, to see what I'm fully capable of—and I think I still have a few special performances in me," she says. "But when the time comes to move on, I'll move on." It will be a tough decision for Flanagan to make, but she's aware of it and knows that eventually, she'll have to make it. That doesn't mean the transition will be easy for Flanagan, but it *will* be less likely to completely throw her off.

PEOPLE LIKE SHALANE FLANAGAN HAVE THE SELF-awareness to understand the power of going all in on something, but also when to pivot to something else. Studies show that those who possess strong internal self-awareness make better decisions, have better personal relationships, are more creative, and have more fulfilling careers.[11] Other research demonstrates that internal self-awareness is associated with improved mental health and general well-being.[12]

When you put all this together, an interesting idea starts to emerge. Maybe the good life is not about trying to achieve some sort of illusory balance. Instead, maybe it's about pursuing your passions fully and harmoniously, but with enough self-awareness to regularly evaluate what you're not pursuing as a result—and make changes if necessary. When it comes to living with passion, it's not about balance. It's about marrying strong harmonious passion, the best kind of passion, with an equally strong self-awareness, a topic we'll turn to next. Doing so trumps balance any day.

When it comes to living with passion, it's not about balance. It's about marrying strong harmonious passion with an equally strong self-awareness. Doing so trumps balance any day.

Passion Practices

- Regardless of what all the self-help books may say, living with passion and being "balanced" are antithetical.
- There are many benefits of living an unbalanced life. Just think about the times you've felt most alive in your own life and answer the question, were you balanced?
- It's OK to be unbalanced, so long as you don't let the inertia of a passionate experience push you forward on autopilot without ever evaluating what you're giving up as a result.
- Don't strive for balance. Instead, strive for the self-awareness that is necessary to evaluate the unique trade-offs that passion requires making in your own life.

7

Self-Awareness and the Power to Choose

From 2000 to 2002, Siri Lindley dominated the sport of triathlon. Within that two-year window, she won an astonishing thirteen International Triathlon Union World Cup races (the crown jewels of the sport) and an overall world championship. No other woman on the planet could combine swimming, biking, and running like Lindley could. But Lindley's rise to prominence in the sport didn't happen overnight. It was built upon years of singular focus and intense passion.

Lindley discovered triathlon in 1993, when, at age twenty-four, she began working her first real job as the member services director at her local YMCA in Worcester, Massachusetts. There she met a group of young women who were crazy about triathlon, which at the time was still an emerging sport. Lindley wanted to learn more about the sport and support her new friends, so she accompanied them to a neighborhood race to serve as cheerleader. She was immediately intrigued by triathlon and the challenge it presented; both the need to master three distinct disciplines and the endurance required to string them together consecutively. Lindley recalls watching the race and being in awe of her friends, but at the same time thinking, *I could do that.* So, like countless others who watch a triathlon and are inspired to give it a shot themselves, Lindley began training.

Lindley brought to her training not only a can-do attitude, but also layers of deep emotional pain from her past and present. Her parents had divorced when she was a young child, her relationship with her biological father was deteriorating, and her relationship with her stepfather was troubled. In addition to these pains, Lindley carried an additional insecurity: at the same time she was getting hooked on triathlon, she was also fully realizing that she was more attracted to women than men. No matter how many boys she dated or forced herself to kiss, this wasn't something she could change. And remember, this was nearly thirty years ago, when the LGBT community faced even more unfair scrutiny and challenges than they do today. In terms of the psychological factors that give rise to intense passion (see chapter 2), Lindley had them all.

Unlike in other sports, in which too much training almost always leads to an overuse injury, the diversity of triathlon allows an athlete to work out furiously for hours upon hours every week with less risk of getting hurt. And that's exactly what Lindley did. Whatever she was lacking in natural talent—she barely finished her first race and struggled awfully in the following few—she made up for twofold with her relentless drive.

From 1995 to 2002, triathlon was Lindley's life. At all hours she was either swimming, biking, or running, or recovering from swimming, biking, or running. Every decision she made was in service of triathlon, from what she ate (a meticulously healthy diet) to where she made her home (first in the mecca of triathlon, Boulder, Colorado; and later at training camps throughout Europe). She lived a solitary, monkish existence. Her entire social life consisted of the athletes she saw during group workouts or at races. Train. Eat. Sleep. Repeat. Lindley was going all in on triathlon. She was *anything but* balanced.

As intense as her passion for triathlon was, it was generally harmonious. Lindley approached triathlon with a mastery mind-set. She incurred both devastating losses (like completely choking during an Olympic qualifying race and missing out on the games) and enormous successes (like winning a world championship). Through it all, she never lost her inner drive or her deep love for the sport. She was focused on the process, possessed an "embrace failure for chronic gains" attitude, and wanted to be the best at getting better—to beat herself—more than anything else. The fact that Lindley appeared to embody the mastery mind-set and the harmonious passion it yields makes it all the more interesting that, at the end of the 2002 season, in the prime of her career and sitting atop the sport, she walked away from triathlon. She quit. And, perhaps even harder to fathom, she wasn't too distressed about the matter.

"Dismantling my fears while building up self-belief allowed me to achieve great things in triathlon," Lindley writes in her memoir, *Surfacing*, "but I no longer needed to seek my self-worth in the sport."[1] As much as she genuinely loved triathlon, Lindley realized that 1) her passion wasn't *all* harmonious, and she may have been relying too heavily on the sport for self-worth, and 2) she was ready to move on from the all-consuming demands of competing. She was ready to direct her passion elsewhere, to devote her energy to other aspects of life. Though she first entered triathlon to, quite literally, run away from parts of her "self," it was through the sport that she cultivated the confidence to more honestly express her whole self.

A big part of being able to leave triathlon, Lindley says, "came from accepting who I was as a person."

The grace and thoughtfulness with which Lindley walked away from triathlon may be even more impressive than anything she accomplished in the sport. She wasn't forced out and she didn't retire because of age or injury. To the contrary, her coach Brett Sutton literally begged Lindley to come back so that she could make a run at Olympic gold in 2004. Four years later, in 2008, he begged her *again* for the same reason. It was clear that Lindley still had much to give in triathlon. But she came to understand that she still had much to give elsewhere, too. Lindley walked away from triathlon because she realized she was ready to. Even though her passion for triathlon was predominantly (though not altogether) harmonious, and even though she could have continued in the sport for many more years, she realized that, at this stage of her life, she was sacrificing too much for triathlon. Lindley's decision to move on from triathlon was neither "good" nor "bad." It was a personal choice, and one with a calculus that shifted over time. What's most important is that it was a *deliberate choice*, and that Lindley didn't just go on with her life on passion-driven autopilot. Lindley's ability to make this deliberate choice required a profound sense of self-awareness.

SELF-AWARENESS IS PERHAPS THE ONLY COUNTERVAILing force strong enough to match the extreme inertia of passion. Possessing it ensures that you can thoughtfully evaluate your passions; that you don't look back twenty years from now and regret how you spent your time. The author Ralph Ellison once wrote, "When I discover who I am, I'll be free."[2] According to the latest research, he's right. Researchers believe that when

Self-awareness allows you to honestly and objectively evaluate your passion and, if necessary, shift course or apply the brakes.

someone is in the midst of a passion, there is often a breakdown in communication between the part of the brain that fuels striving (the striatum) and the part of the brain that controls and regulates striving (the prefrontal cortex). The only known way to regain this connection, and in doing so regain control of how you pursue your passion, is through deep introspection and the self-awareness it yields. Self-awareness allows you to honestly and objectively evaluate your passion and, if necessary, shift course or apply the brakes.

It's important to understand that gaining astute self-awareness does not always result in someone moving on from a passion like Lindley did. Many of those who are responsible for propelling humanity forward—including the best scientists, physicians, artists, athletes, and entrepreneurs—are self-aware, yet they still continue to devote their entire lives to their passions. Self-awareness simply empowers you to evaluate and reevaluate how you pursue your passions. It gives you the

Self-awareness simply empowers you to evaluate and reevaluate how you pursue your passions. It gives you the power to choose if and when to pull back from a passion—or, alternatively, if and when to push forward, perhaps with even more fire and drive.

power to choose if and when to pull back from a passion—or, alternatively, if and when to push forward, perhaps with even more fire and drive. Passion may require forfeiting balance, but it need not require forfeiting control of your life. Self-awareness keeps you in control.

KNOW THYSELF

Self-awareness represents the ability to make accurate assessments of your beliefs, values, emotions, and behaviors, and to be cognizant of how you are expressing them in any given context. It gives you the power to rationally and clearly see a situation and your role in it, preventing you from being blinded by powerful emotions. It provides you with the ability to choose what is important to you based on your core values and beliefs, not based on neurochemically charged states. In a sense, it allows you to remain in control of your destiny, preventing you from acting automatically and being swept up in the momentum of the moment.

You'd think we would know the person with whom we spend every minute—our "self"—better than anyone. After all, we are a privileged witness to each and every one of our inner thoughts, and we have been since the beginning of our lives. Yet research out of the University of Washington in St. Louis, Missouri, shows that our friends, and in some circumstances, even strangers, tend to know us better than we know ourselves. In one study, researchers had subjects use a validated psychological survey to evaluate their personality traits and tendencies like anxiousness, intelligence, and gregariousness. Then the participants were asked to complete a self-assessment, appraising themselves on the same traits and tendencies that were evaluated in the survey. The researchers didn't stop there. They were interested not only in how well individuals could self-assess but also in how accurate the assessments of outside observers—friends and total strangers—would be. On average, when compared to the validated survey, the friends' ratings were far more accurate than the participants' assessments of themselves. For more polarizing traits like hubris, even the ratings of strangers, after having observed someone for only a few minutes, were more accurate than the subjects' ratings of themselves.[3] These studies do not mean that we can never come to more accurately evaluate ourselves. Some people truly know themselves, offering self-assessments that are dead-on accurate. It's just that getting to this point takes time and deliberate practice. No different from a close relationship with anyone else, you need to work at having a close relationship with yourself.

Seeing ourselves clearly is so challenging because our view is often clouded by emotions. This is especially true when we are looking at ourselves in the context of things that make us tick, and none more so than our passions. We can get so wrapped up in whatever it is we are doing that it becomes damn near impossible to make any sort of objective or honest evaluation. This is why individuals suffering from maladaptive "addictions," most notably eating disorders, struggle to recognize that anything is wrong. They literally look in the mirror and fail to see a problem. Not eating isn't necessarily the pathological part, but the incorrect self-assessment, the inability to see reality, is. Yes, this is an extreme example, but as we discussed earlier, there is much in common between someone with a damning addiction, someone going for a gold medal, and someone trying to build a billion-dollar company. In each case, neurochemically charged feelings can take over and obscure one's view of reality. Perhaps this is why eating disorders are so common in serious athletes, a long-known (and studied) truth that gained attention during the 2018 Winter Olympics when breakout figure skater Adam Rippon came out publicly about

No different from a close relationship with anyone else, you need to work at having a close relationship with yourself.

his battle with an eating disorder.[4] It's true that lots of athletes struggle with eating disorders because they think being lighter will make them perform better. But presumably their underlying brain chemistry and personality—and their singular focus on their pursuit and "do whatever it takes" mind-set—fuel the fire, too. The narrowing function of wholeheartedly pursuing a passion to the exclusion of almost everything else is not too different from the narrowing function of an eating disorder.

Fortunately, there are a few practical strategies that can help us gain the self-awareness we need to see ourselves and evaluate our situations more clearly. These strategies help us stay in control of our passions and ensure that we are consciously and thoughtfully *choosing* how we engage in them.

PASSION PRACTICES

- The inertia of passion can become overpowering.
- The best way to counter this inertia is through keen self-awareness.
- Self-awareness helps to ensure that you are deliberately *choosing* if and how to pursue your passion; that you remain in control of your passion, and thus remain in control of your life.
- Though it seems like you'd know yourself better than anyone, that's not the case. Becoming self-aware doesn't happen automatically. Rather, it requires intention and proactive strategies.

SELF-DISTANCING

Rebecca Rusch is arguably the best adventure racer alive. She's won a slew of world championships in sports ranging from whitewater rafting to mountain biking to cross-country skiing. She's also won preeminent events in orienteering, a sport in which participants are dropped off in the middle of nowhere, often in the middle of the night, and must navigate their way back to a specified point. Rusch has even ridden her bike to the top of Mount Kilimanjaro. She's an extreme outlier in a small community of extreme outliers. A large part of her success lies in her ability to remain self-aware in emotionally charged situations.

Given what she does, it's not uncommon for Rusch to find herself in dark spots; perhaps she's lost on an unmarked trail in the middle of a 200-mile bike ride, or running out of food on a mountain ridge at two a.m. When she's in these situations, Rusch creates space between her thoughts and feelings by pretending she's giving advice to a friend. This strategy allows her to see more clearly and think more rationally in the midst of an emotionally fraught moment. "Pretending I'm thinking about a friend rather than myself," she says, "almost always provides me with more clarity and insight about what to do in a tricky situation."[5] Although you may never find yourself in the circumstances that Rusch does, her practice is a valuable one. It's a great way to gain self-awareness in just about any situation where emotional inertia is at play.

Take, for example, a study conducted at the University of Waterloo in Ontario, Canada. In the study, psychologist Igor Grossmann divided one hundred students, all of whom were in long-term relationships, into two groups. The first group of students was prompted to imagine, in vivid color, that they had been cheated on by their significant other. The second group was presented with the same prompt, only they were asked to imagine that it was their best friend who had been cheated on, not themselves. Immediately after going through this exercise, both groups of students answered questions designed to evaluate their ability to handle the situation wisely (e.g., seeing both perspectives, having the ability to compromise, assessing multiple solutions). The students who had imagined their friend in the situation scored much higher on "wise reasoning," or the ability to appraise the situation with accuracy and wisdom, than those who imagined themselves in the situation.[6] Similar studies show that when individuals think or journal in third person rather than in first person—for example, "John is running into challenges with his start-up that seem insurmountable" versus "I am running into challenges with my start-up that seem insurmountable"—they also evaluate themselves and their situations more clearly.[7]

Collectively referred to as "self-distancing," practices like those outlined above allow us to remove our emotional selves from highly charged situations, paving the way for more thoughtful insight and subsequent decision-making. The psychologists Özlem Ayduk and Ethan Kross, who have studied the effects of self-distancing across contexts, write that the practice "leads people to focus relatively less on *recounting* the emotionally evocative details of their experience (i.e., what happened) and relatively more on *recasting* it in ways that promote insight and closure. This shift in the content of people's thoughts about their past experiences, in turn, leads to lower levels of emotional reactivity."[8] In other words, when we take ourselves out of the picture, we often gain a much fuller and more holistic view of it; a view that promotes thinking alongside feeling and yields greater wisdom.

Regularly evaluate your passions as if they belong to someone else. What would you say to that other person? Would you tell them to keep pushing, or perhaps to push even harder? Or would you tell them, like the triathlete Siri Lindley told herself, to pull back, that the trade-offs they are making in order to pursue their passion are too great? In many ways, reading this book serves as a self-distancing exercise. Merely gaining a better understanding of passion—its origins, its underlying causes, how it can go awry, how it can be harmonious, and the costs that come with pursuing it—should help you reflect on how best to live with it yourself.

> *Regularly evaluate your passions as if they belong to someone else. What would you say to that other person? Would you tell them to keep pushing, or perhaps to push even harder? Or would you tell them to pull back, that the trade-offs they are making in order to pursue their passion are too great?*

Self-distancing helps us gain self-awareness by zooming out of our own selves and situations, even if only a little bit. It allows our more rational, thinking brain to emerge and flex its muscle in circumstances that are laden with passion. If self-distancing is about zooming out just a bit, then what happens when we zoom *way* out?

PERSPECTIVE

Looking down on Earth from over two hundred thousand miles away, astronauts can't help but gain some perspective. They report discovering a new appreciation of "their world" versus "the world," and they begin to think of everything from the passage of time to their own personal achievements quite differently. They obtain insight and clarity that is hard to come by on Earth. Astronaut Ron Garan, who has traveled over 71,000,000 miles and orbited Earth 2,842 times, calls this "orbital perspective."[9] The scientific community calls it the *overview effect*, or a cognitive shift in awareness reported by some astronauts during spaceflight, most often while viewing Earth from orbit.[10]

When we are pursuing a passion, however, our perspective is anything but orbital. We are completely zoomed in. Our world narrows and our focus constricts so that our seeing, thinking, and feeling are dominated by the activity that we are passionate about. Living life in such a zoomed-in state allows us to accomplish incredible things, like winning triathlon world championships, discovering cures for diseases, or writing beautiful symphonies and concertos. It gives rise to the special kind of Quality, when you become one with your activity, that we discussed in chapter 5. But it also prevents us from seeing a broader picture. When we lose perspective—when all we can see is our passion—we lose the ability to choose what we want to do with our lives. It's like a fish that knows nothing exists beyond life underwater. This sounds trite, but it's true. When we are really going for something, for better or worse, passion all too easily takes over. In order to prevent ourselves from succumbing to passion-driven autopilot and to reclaim at least a modicum of say in the matter of how we spend our time, attention, and energy—that is to say, how we spend our lives—we must recalibrate our perspective.

Unfortunately, barring dramatic improvements in technology, few people reading this book today will travel to outer space. But that doesn't mean there aren't other ways to broaden our view. Psychological research suggests that it isn't necessarily the specific act of looking down on Earth from outer space that results in orbital perspective, but rather the unmatched awe that accompanies it. Luckily, we can experience awe and the perspective it brings without ever leaving Earth.

University of California Berkeley psychology professor Dacher Keltner defines awe as the sense of wonder we feel "in the presence of something vast that transcends our understanding of the world."[11] Yet Keltner says we need not be looking down at Earth from the moon, or even standing in the middle of the Grand Canyon, to feel it. In fact, Keltner's research has found that there are a handful of easily accessible experiences that tend to elicit awe in most people.[12]

> When we lose perspective—when all we can see is our passion—we lose the ability to choose what we want to do with our lives.

- Immersing oneself in lush, natural environments.*
- Watching the sunset, stargazing, or observing a full moon.
- Viewing artistic works.
- Listening to music that moves you.
- Looking for examples of extraordinary human kindness (e.g., spending a day volunteering in a homeless shelter).
- Observing a craftsperson at work using their unbelievable skill (e.g., watching LeBron James playing basketball or Bette Midler acting on Broadway).

All these examples expose us to phenomena that are beyond what we normally comprehend in day-to-day life. These awesome experiences tend to make us ponder the grandness of time, space, or beauty. Works that move us help reshape our perspective. Following these and other awe-inspiring experi-

---

* Anyone who has read the book or seen the movie *Wild* understands the perspective shift that author Cheryl Strayed underwent when she listened to her mom and "put [herself] in the way of [nature's] beauty." If you aren't familiar with *Wild*, we recommend you read the book and/or watch the film. It's a great example of how time in nature can help someone gain perspective and acquire keen self-awareness.

ences, we can't help but view ourselves and our pursuits against a larger backdrop. Feeling awe forces us, even if only for a brief moment, to zoom out of our own lives and passions and realize that there are things beyond them. "A long view of time," writes the author Krista Tippett in her beautiful book *Becoming Wise*, "can replenish our sense of ourselves and the world."[13]

Similar to self-distancing, when we are in the midst of an awesome experience, we gain not only perspective but also the clarity required to more objectively evaluate what we call our true selves—what lies at our core beyond the pursuit of our passions—and how we are spending our time and energy. This is a type of clarity that is often absent when we are heads-down pursuing a passion.

Sadly, science is demonstrating the great value of awe at a time when our culture is becoming increasingly awe-deprived. Thus, we must deliberately and actively seek it out. Here is Dacher Keltner:

> Adults spend more and more time working and commuting and less time outdoors and with other people. So often our gaze is fixed on our smartphones rather than noticing the wonders and beauty of the natural world or witnessing acts of kindness, which also inspire awe. Attendance at arts events—live music, theater, museums and galleries—has dropped in recent years. This goes for children, too: Arts and music programs in schools are being dismantled; time spent outdoors and for unstructured exploration is being sacrificed for résumé-building activities. At the same time, our culture has become more *individualistic*, more *narcissistic*, more *materialistic*, and *less connected to others* . . . Don't underestimate the power of goosebumps—actively seek out the experiences that nurture your own hunger for

awe, be it through appreciating the trees in your neighborhood, a complex piece of music, patterns of wind on water, the person who presses on against all odds, or the everyday nobility of others.[14]

There is nothing like a walk in a redwood forest or a view from atop a mountain to remind us that we are small and the world is big. When we expose ourselves to awe, we gain the perspective to make more thoughtful, fully conscious decisions about how we want to channel our energy, engage in our respective passions, and make big life choices. Although the latest science on the power of self-distancing and awe is fascinating, wise minds have understood this to be true for centuries. Writing some two thousand years ago, the Stoic philosopher Seneca advised that people "place before [their] mind's eye the vast spread of time's abyss, and consider the universe; and then contrast our so called life with infinity."[15] We'd all be wise to more regularly follow his advice.

When we expose ourselves to awe, we gain the perspective to make more thoughtful, fully conscious decisions about how we want to channel our energy, engage in our respective passions, and make big life choices.

MEDITATION

Another way to create space between your thoughts (and the feelings tangled up in them) and yourself is through meditation, particularly a variety called mindfulness. Mindfulness meditation is the practice of sitting or lying down and focusing on your breath. When thoughts or feelings arise, you acknowledge them without judgment—like clouds passing through the sky—and return your focus to the sensation of your breath. Mindfulness is as simple and as hard as that.

There is a common misconception that "the point" of mindfulness meditation is to enter a relaxed, Zen-like state. Arriving at such a state is possible, and for most people the experience is quite pleasant, but that's not really the goal of meditation. There is no goal other than simply sitting and being with your breath, letting whatever thoughts and feelings arise come and go, watching them float by and experiencing them without judgment.

And yet, if you practice regularly—ideally building up to twenty minutes or more per day*—after a month (or a few months), something interesting may begin to happen: You're liable to start seeing your thoughts and feelings as separate from your "self." You gain a sense of a deeper and wiser observing self—what some meditation teachers simply call awareness—and some distance between it and everything else that your mind creates. Resting in this awareness can be a beautiful experience.

Another way to think about mindfulness meditation is this: Imagine the difference between being in a fast-paced action movie versus *watching* a fast-paced action movie. In the former, you are fully in the story, constantly reacting to what's happening with hardly any time or space to analyze it. Go. Go. Go. In the latter, even though the movie may be very intense, and even though at times you may truly feel like you've been sucked into it, you still feel a bit safer and retain the ability to be more thoughtful knowing that you're merely watching. When you practice meditation, you cultivate the ability to step out of the

---

* For more on the practice of meditation, see our first book, *Peak Performance*. If you're looking for a deeper dive, see *Full Catastrophe Living* and *Wherever You Go, There You Are* by Jon Kabat-Zinn and *Mindfulness in Plain English* by Bhante Gunaratana.

movie—that is, the endless stream of thoughts and feelings in your head and body—and instead watch from afar. And it is this watching from afar that offers you the ability to step outside the inertia of whatever it is you are caught up in so you can deliberately and perhaps even wisely *choose* what to do next, instead of being pulled along on autopilot.

Mindfulness, writes the great meditation teacher Jon Kabat-Zinn, allows you to "perceive with clarity the path you are actually on and the direction in which you are going . . . [so that] maybe you will be in a better position to chart a course for yourself that is truer to your inner being—a soul path, a path with heart, *your* path with a capital P."[16]

THERE IS ONE FINAL WAY TO RELIABLY GAIN PERSPECTIVE, and it's perhaps even more powerful than any of the strategies mentioned above: thinking about death. There is no greater reminder that our time is finite, no better mechanism to focus us in on what we really want out of life, than reflecting on our own impending end. Sometimes this is forced upon us. In 2015, when Brad was twenty-nine years old, his close friend Jim,* who was twenty-eight at the time, was diagnosed with stage-IV lymphoma. This completely rocked Brad's world. He had observed the death of other people he had been close to, but they were all much older. The very real and devastatingly high probability that his friend and contemporary Jim might soon die not only deeply saddened Brad, but also brought him face-to-face with his own mortality unlike anything else had before. (You can only imagine how Jim felt.) During this period, among other things, Brad realized that he wanted to spend his days writ-

---

* This name has been changed to protect the identity of Brad's friend.

ing; that it was writing that really made him tick, that a good day was a day spent writing. Brad made very real changes in his life so he could spend more time writing, significantly cutting down his consulting workload, in effect turning a full-time job with many potential promotions into a part-time gig, and also shedding many "hobbies" that weren't really fulfilling. With his own mortality at the forefront of his mind, Brad was more easily able to focus on what mattered most. (Thankfully, Jim is now a cancer survivor and has a good prognosis. He even got married during the period of time we were writing this book.)

At one point or another, all of us will have experiences that make us confront our own mortality. But we shouldn't necessarily wait for them. We should somewhat regularly reflect on mortality instead. Many people don't like thinking about death because it makes them uneasy, but one of our strongest recommendations in this book is that you should do it more often. Keeping death at the forefront of your mind is one of the best ways to ensure you live the life you want to live.

The Buddhist practice of the Five Remembrances is a practical way to gain the perspective that death affords. Once a week, perhaps during your Friday-afternoon commute, devote just five minutes to reflecting on the fact that:

1. You are of the nature to grow old.
2. You are of the nature to have ill health.
3. You are of the nature to die.
4. All that is dear to you is of the nature to change.
5. Your actions are your only true belongings; they are the ground upon which you stand.

This reflection can be very uncomfortable, but it is extremely powerful. It goes a long way to ensure you are consciously choosing how you spend your time and energy, that you never lose sight of the fact that time is both finite and the most precious resource there is. Another way to think of this practice is that you want to go to bed every night being content with what you did that day, as if you don't know whether you'll wake up the next morning (which, in reality, none of us do). How do you want to be remembered? What actions do you want to contribute to the world?

In addition to practicing the Five Remembrances, you can also become a student of mortality by reading books that intimately explore the topic.* It's worth reiterating that the cost (in unease and discomfort) of reflecting on death is great. But the cost of not doing so, of *actually* getting an awful diagnosis and realizing you didn't live the life you wanted to, is far greater. As Seneca explained, it's all too easy to hum along, living without ever thinking about the one consistent truth of life: that your time is always running out. "Life will cause no commotion to remind you of its swiftness, but glide on quietly," he writes in *On the Shortness of Life: Life Is Long If You Know How to Use It*. "What will be the outcome? You have been preoccupied while life hastens on. Meanwhile death will arrive, and you have no choice in making yourself available for that."[17]

Keeping death at the forefront of your mind is one of the best ways to ensure you live the life you want to live.

Centuries later, in her memoir on living with and dying from cancer, the late poet Nina Riggs wrote that "living with a terminal disease is like walking on a tightrope over an insanely scary abyss. But living without a terminal disease is also like walking

---

* Three recommendations are *When Breath Becomes Air* by the late Paul Kalanithi, *The Bright Hour* by the late Nina Riggs, and *Death* by Todd May.

over an insanely scary abyss, only with some fog or cloud cover obscuring the depths a little more."[18]

Nothing makes us more self-aware or focuses us on what really matters more than realizing what we experience as our "self" won't be around forever. That we are each just a speck of dust passing through the universe. Reminding ourselves of this is the ultimate form of zooming out.

THIS CHAPTER BEGAN BY MAKING THE POINT THAT THE art of living with the best kind of passion over a lifetime relies heavily on self-awareness. When you are in the throes of a passion, your ability to see beyond it often deteriorates. As a result, you lose the power to *choose* how you want to spend your time and energy. Your passion controls you, rather than you controlling it. The key to protecting yourself from the intense inertia of passion lies in cultivating self-awareness. Ironically, the best way to do so is to step back from yourself. Regularly self-distancing (thinking about a situation as if a friend is experiencing it, rather than yourself, or thinking/journaling in third person) and deliberately gaining perspective (by exposing yourself to awe, meditating, or reflecting on mortality) are two of the most effective ways to remain self-aware and maintain your ability to choose, even in the midst of pursuing a passion.

It's important to remember that there is no such thing as a "right" choice, and that the choices you make may change over time.* Oftentimes, you'll choose to continue throwing yourself fully into a passion. And so long as it's a conscious choice,

---

* Studies find that as people grow older, they tend to shift focus from pursuing activities to spending time with family and long-standing friends.

it's yours to make, and often a wonderful decision. Few things make you feel more alive than pursuing a passion harmoniously. But what happens if, like triathlete Siri Lindley, you realize it's time to move on, time to retire? Or, if your passion is a physical one, your body makes that decision for you? Or if your employer or profession makes that decision for you? Worse yet, what happens if your passion is loving another person, and he or she dies? How can we move forward, with both grace and grit, from our passions? We turn to this question next, in chapter 8.

PASSION PRACTICES

- One of the best ways to gain the self-awareness required to productively live with passion is to step outside your "self."
  - Pretend a friend is in the same situation you are and then give advice to him or her about what to do.
  - Journal about the big decisions in your life in the third person and then reflect on what you wrote and how you felt when you were writing it.
- Another way to gain self-awareness is to ensure you regularly take a greater perspective.
  - Expose yourself to awe-evoking experiences as often as you can.
    - › Immerse yourself in lush, natural environments.
    - › Watch the sunset, stargaze, or observe a full moon.
    - › View artistic works.
    - › Listen to music that moves you.

> › Look for examples of extraordinary human kindness in daily life.
> › Bear witness to a craftsperson at work using their unbelievable skill.

- Meditate.
- Become a student of mortality: Every so often, reflect on your own mortality by practicing the Five Remembrances and/or reading about death and dying.
- Becoming more self-aware is so important because it affords you the ability to evaluate the trade-offs inherent to living a passionate life, and allows you to *choose* how to channel your passion.

8

Moving On
How to Transition from a Passion with Grace and Grit

W hether we choose to or are forced to, moving on from something or someone we are passionate about can be one of the hardest challenges of our lives. Although it is desirable to keep our identity separate from the accomplishments and external validation that may be the result of our passions, it's nearly impossible to keep our identity separate from our passions themselves. As we discussed in chapter 5, when we adopt the mastery mind-set, our passions often transition from a verb (something we do) to a noun (someone we are). We go from writing to being a writer. From running to being a runner. From loving to being a lover. So, then: How can we lose our passion without losing our self?

It's not easy. Many individuals who move on from their respective passions (even those who do so by choice, under their own volition) fall into a depression or get hooked on destructive addictions like drugs, drinking, or gambling. This is as true for a recent widow as it is for an Olympian who must hang up her racing shoes or an artist who must shut down his gallery. It's a double whammy. We must deal with not only losing a large part of our identity, of what makes us who we are, but also losing something into which we could channel our intense drive—which, as you learned earlier, is in and of itself a product of hard-to-change biology and psychology. Moving on can create a void.

TO ABBY WAMBACH, ARGUABLY THE GREATEST AMERIcan soccer player ever, soccer was so much more than a game; it was the outlet for her rage and insecurity. Wambach, one of six siblings, was constantly in a battle for her parents' attention growing up. Wambach is also gay, which, as it meant for so many other young homosexual men and women (including Siri Lindley, who you read about in the previous chapter), unfortunately meant questioning whether her social circle would accept her. As an adolescent, it would be fair to say that Wambach's identity was fragile. But she had sports. "Feeling like an athlete," she writes in her memoir, *Forward*, "is your only authentic identity, a sum total far greater than all of your parts."[1] No different from Lindley with triathlon, Wambach threw every bit of herself into soccer.

But by the time she hit her mid-thirties, Wambach's body simply had nothing left to give. Like so many other great athletes, she was no longer able to manage injuries and chronic conditions that were once manageable, and she was left with little choice but to step away from the sport she loved and retire. She struggled mightily to leave the game to which she had devoted her life. She had issues with gambling, drinking, and substance abuse. "The various [painkillers] I took to do my job, I now needed to live my life," admits Wambach. "Retirement is not peaches and cream . . . People don't talk about the transitions enough, the hard bits of life."[2] What's fascinating is that Wambach's story closely mirrors that of one of her contemporaries, the Olympic swimmer Michael Phelps. Phelps also had a rough upbringing and destructive episodes involving gambling, drinking, and substance abuse when he first tried to retire from swimming. This isn't surprising. When the stability of your identity and the structure of your life disappear at the same time, it's easy to see how chaos often ensues.

Even so, not everyone who moves on from a passion suffers greatly. Some people are able to move forward in a more hopeful manner. It's not that they don't miss and sometimes long for their passion. It's just that they are not *consumed* by missing and longing for their passion.

Take the example of marketing guru Chris Lukezic. Imagine for a moment that you are one of the best in the world at what you do. You get to travel the globe and compete for glory in an activity you've loved since you were a teenager—and you get paid to do it. That's the position Lukezic found himself in during the early part of his career as a professional runner, when he finished seventh at the World Indoor Track Championships. Shortly after his great performance at the world championships, however, and while still at the top of his game, he announced his retirement from professional running at the age of twenty-six.

When the stability of your identity and the structure of your life disappear at the same time, it's easy to see how chaos often ensues.

His decision shocked the running community. Why would a young, healthy, sponsored athlete retire at such a young age? Was Lukezic overtrained or burnt out?

To the contrary: He was following the same path that had led him to the sport of running a decade earlier, and doing something we touched on earlier in this book. Lukezic was just following his interests. In reflecting on his decision, Lukezic recalls, "My heart has always been pulled in a million different fragmented directions. Running was never the only interest I had, but it was the only interest I pursued. And I did so with the entirety of my heart." In moving on, Lukezic wasn't bitter, but content in the effort he had put into running. Now he wanted to put the same effort into a new challenge. Of course he missed

> *What people who move forward from their passions in a productive manner have in common is unyielding ownership and authorship of their stories.*

running, but he knew deep down inside that his time to move forward had come. As he told the running website Letsrun.com at the time, "The Mondo oval [tracks] of Europe were like the curvy pin-ups you drool over as a teenager. Eventually, you fall out of love with Cindy Crawford because, well, frankly, you realize she's 20 years older than you and by the time you're ready to marry her, she'll be nearly 50. My desires have changed."

Two months before calling it quits on his running career, Lukezic had sent an impassioned letter to a start-up company that had captured his attention because it was involved in the interest that was capturing his mind at the time: travel. Outlining his enthusiasm and desire to join the young team, Lukezic wrote, "[The company] will help us all to rethink our notions of community in the virtual, local, and global realms . . . [It has] injected real human experience into the travel process."

When he announced his retirement on a popular running message board, Lukezic was widely ridiculed, with anonymous posters proclaiming, "Chucking it all to join a company with a circa 1995 home page, that seems like a poor choice."

Fortunately, Lukezic didn't listen to the naysayers. He followed his interest and took ownership of his decision, ready to shed his old identity as a runner and throw all that drive and determination into other passions. In 2009, he began the next chapter of his story and joined Airbnb as employee number six.

WRITE YOUR STORY

What people like Lukezic who move forward from their passions in a productive manner have in common is unyielding ownership and authorship of their stories. Your inner narrative, or the story you tell yourself about yourself, provides the lens through which you see, make sense of, and navigate the world. How you craft it is the key to moving on from a passion productively.

In the 1960s, the Nobel Prize–winning neuropsychologist Roger Sperry began studying individuals who, in an effort to treat their severe epilepsy, had had their corpus callosum severed (a popular treatment at the time). The corpus callosum is a broad band of nerve fibers that joins the two hemispheres of the brain. It's like a bridge by which our more analytical and logical left brain communicates with our more creative and emotional right brain. When the corpus callosum is severed, so, too, is communication between the hemispheres of the brain.

Sperry would flash commands (e.g., "walk," "draw," "sit down") to either the right or left side of a subject's visual field. Human neurology is such that what we see in the left visual field gets picked up by the right brain, and what we see in the right visual field gets picked up by the left brain. When Sperry flashed a command in the left visual field so that it was picked up by the right brain, the subjects would execute the command (they would walk, draw, or sit down) but have no idea why. That's because the right side of the brain doesn't have the capacity to explain or rationalize. It simply directs actions and perceives emotions.

What's fascinating is that, without fail, Sperry's subjects would always create some sort of story to explain their action. For instance, if Sperry flashed the command "walk," the subjects might say they walked because they needed to stretch their legs, or get a drink of water, or because their spouse wanted them to get some more exercise. In other words, even though they had no idea why they were walking, they made up a story to justify it. (If they truly knew why they had begun walking, they would have said it was because Sperry flashed a card commanding them to do so!) In later studies, the same effect was observed for emotional states. If a tragic picture was flashed in the left visual field (so it would be picked up by the right brain), subjects would make up all manner of stories for why they felt sad. Sperry's research demonstrated that stories are central to our nature. We literally cannot do or feel anything without creating an accompanying narrative. One of the defining features of the human species is that we are programmed to construct stories to make meaning of our lives. Without such stories, we feel lost.[3]

Some sixty years after Sperry's groundbreaking research, we are just now beginning to learn that the stories we tell ourselves don't just describe our actions and feelings after the fact, but also influence our actions and feelings prior to life events and as they are unfolding. Carol Dweck, a psychology professor at Stanford University, has found that changing students' internal narratives for why they succeed or fail influences their academic performance. When students transition from telling themselves a "fixed" story ("I was born with a certain level of intelligence and it cannot change") to a "growth" story ("The human brain can grow and, with practice and hard work, become smarter over time"), their attitude, effort, and grades all improve. In other words, when their story changes, they change with it.[4]

Additional research shows that our personal narratives are particularly important when it comes to resilience. In a 2015 study conducted at the University of Michigan's Department of Psychiatry and Comprehensive Depression Center, researchers focused on the spouses of individuals who had been deployed to war zones. Upon entering the study, many of the spouses had internal narratives about their significant other's deployment that were dominated by negative thoughts, such as helplessness, feeling overwhelmed, and feeling unsupported. These individuals also had high rates of depression. Over the course of two months, the spouses who had negative stories were counseled on how to change their stories to include more positive attributes (e.g., hope, self-competence, feeling supported). One month after this intervention, the spouses who had edited their stories reported fewer symptoms of depression, higher levels of social support, and greater overall life satisfaction.[5] Nothing had changed about the deployment status of their significant others. All that had changed were the stories they told themselves about the deployment of their significant others. In the words of Vincent Harding, a civil rights leader who worked with Martin Luther King Jr. to develop the premise of nonvio-

Stories are central to our nature. We literally cannot do or feel anything without creating an accompanying narrative. Without such stories, we feel lost.

lent protest, "there is something deeply built into us that needs story itself . . . we cannot become really true human beings for ourselves without story."[6]

When the time comes to move on from a passion, it is imperative that you take control of your story. You must tell yourself a story about yourself that goes beyond seeing your passion as the sole source of your fulfillment and identity. It's not that you should forget about your passion completely; in fact, quite the opposite. You should recognize and accept how your passion changed you and then constructively integrate those insights into a forever unfolding story, a story that has future chapters. The word *constructively* is key. Like the military spouses, you shouldn't focus on the negatives: what you lost when you lost your passion. Rather, you should focus on the positives: what you gained from your passion; the underlying characteristics that fueled it and that can now be directed elsewhere; and everything else that you still have to live for. While the following examples are overly simplified, they are meant to highlight the differences in these approaches:

- "My time as a competitive athlete is over, and that's all I've ever done. What will I do now?"
- "Through athletics, I developed a fierce competitive drive and I learned how to be comfortable with being uncomfortable. I can use both of these assets in pursuing a job at a start-up company, or perhaps even coaching other athletes."

- "My wife of forty years passed away. How can I go on, what do I have to live for? My life is over."
- "I am deeply saddened by my loss, but forever thankful for the memories we created together. I have friends and family

who will support me through this time and continue to love me. As a matter of fact, my wife lives on through all those people."

- "My company failed and there's simply no way I will be able to get funding for anything else again. The work that gave my life meaning is over."
- "My company failed but I learned so many valuable lessons along the way. I'll forever be able to apply these lessons across all areas of my life. I can also use this as an opportunity to take stock of what I really want out of life, and spend more time with my wife and kids."

Make no mistake: We are not encouraging delusional thinking nor lying to oneself. An overly rosy view of the world is neither conducive to long-term happiness nor health. When you lose a passion, you *should* feel pain and grief. What we are encouraging, however, is consciously choosing to encode in your memory, via story, the positive aspects of your passion that you can take with you and build upon in the future. Doing so not only makes you feel better in the short term, but, perhaps more important, also helps you to find complementary activities that will fulfill you in the long term.

When the time comes to move on from a passion, it is imperative that you take control of your story. You must tell yourself a story about yourself that goes beyond seeing your passion as the sole source of your fulfillment and identity.

Much like with Carol Dweck's students, there is great benefit in transitioning from a fixed and negative story to a more positive, flexible, and forward-looking one. When you do so, you open yourself up to the world and are likely to find other pursuits that will bring you joy and fulfillment. You identify what it is about your passion that you most loved; what skills and capabilities you've gained; and what new and different experiences you are seeking. In combination, these insights will help you find whatever it is that will fulfill the next stage of your life. In a sense, you don't move on from a passion. You move forward from one.

There are a variety of ways people strive to help individuals move forward from their passions—from grief counseling to Olympic "transition out of sport" courses to the informal advice one gets from friends when they retire. Unfortunately, however well-intentioned they may be, most of these attempts spend the lion's share of their time *telling* people what to do. (For example: "find a job immediately," "start volunteering," "travel," "surround yourself with friends.") We believe it is far more effective for individuals to create *their own* unique, forward-looking stories. Doing so in a supportive environment/community helps.

When moving on from a passion in your own life, it can be tempting to quickly turn to something or someone new to fill the void. But it's often better to pause and open up some space during which you can reflect on what it is you loved about your passion, what you think you'll miss most, and how you'd like your own unique story—the story of your life—to unfold. These liminal spaces are inherently rife with uncertainty. Inhabiting them can be uncomfortable. But they are critical frontiers, opportunities to search inside yourself, to shape your future. Take the time to look inward. When the formal transitional programs end and all your wonderful advice-giving friends go back to living their own lives, you'll still have a constructive and intimate guide to follow. You won't feel lost.

AFTER ENDURING A PARTICULARLY LOW PERIOD THAT IN-cluded being arrested for driving under the influence of alcohol,

Wambach realized she was lost and had to regain control of her story. Her life literally depended on it. In her memoir, *Forward*, she cites a metaphor that a friend relayed to her to capture the difficulty of transitions and retirement. "Trapeze artists are so amazing in so many ways," Wambach's friend says, "because they are grounded to one rung for a long time, and in order to get to the other rung they have to let go. What makes them so brilliant and beautiful and courageous and strong is that they execute flips in the middle. The middle is their magic. If you're brave enough to let go of that first rung, you can create your own magic in the middle."[7]

Wambach is still working on creating her own magic, but she's making progress. In *Forward*, Wambach tells a story from a recent vacation in France: A woman stops her and says, "Are you Abby Wambach? The soccer player?" *I'm in France!* Wambach thinks. *Are you serious?* Wambach writes that her ego "can't help but preen" as she acknowledges that yes, she is a soccer player. But then in her mind Wambach corrects both herself and the woman. *I'm not a soccer player anymore*, she thinks. Yet it's not long before Wambach realizes that perhaps the woman is right after all. "Soccer is no longer what I do," she writes, "but it will always be a part of who I am, an indispensable thread of my past. I can't deny it any more than I can deny the other labels [I've claimed]: fraud, rebel, wife, advocate, addict, failure, human—all of them. They'll always be there, stitched into my psyche, even as I make room for new labels, ones I've yet to discover and claim."[8]

WAMBACH'S STORY HITS PARTICULARLY CLOSE TO ONE of us, Steve. Since the age of fourteen, Steve largely identified himself as a runner. It wasn't just that he ran, it's that everyone he knew saw him as a runner, too. His entire being, both internal and external, was tied up in the sport, in no small part because he was quite good at it. This interconnectedness between sport and identity only intensified when, at the age of eighteen, Steve ran a 4:01 mile, at the time the sixth-fastest high school mile run in US history. In those 241 seconds, it seemed that Steve sealed his fate to be forever known as a runner. For a while, this wasn't such a big deal. If anything, Steve reveled in the accomplishment and subsequent attention that resulted from a vast body of hard work. But as his running career progressed and he failed to improve upon his early indicators of talent, his identity as a runner became a burden.

For years, everywhere Steve went, he'd be introduced as a runner, or the guy who ran the mile in 4:01. It was as if he had those two facts tattooed across his forehead. No matter what else he accomplished—on the road or off—he felt stuck. It got to the point where Steve didn't want to show up to a track meet or road race, even if he was just participating for fun, because inevitably the announcer or someone else at the meet would remind him of his singular identity as a runner and the fact that he hadn't improved since high school. With each mention of his past, anxiety and fear would surge through his body, making him instantly want to transport anywhere else. Steve's identity became a heavy weight on his shoulders and heart because, at least in his mind, he could never live up to it. Instead of taking pride in the fact that he had had such great early success in the sport, it became a source of shame, representing Steve's failure to reach his own—and, perhaps even more burdensome, others'—perceived potential.

Even as he grew older and more mature, and attempted to transition from running to other fields like coaching and writing, it took years for Steve to come to terms with who he is. In order to realize that he wasn't defined by any one moment or any one activity, he had to actively rewrite his internal story, in essence convincing himself that he had diverse abilities and skills—beyond just making four fast laps around a track—to offer to the world. Ironically, as he gained notoriety in fields beyond running, he saw the same overly simple and singular "identity" stereotyping being applied. Now instead of the "runner," he became the "coach" or "scientist" or "author." Whatever the label, the process of stereotyping was the same. Steve came to learn that he had to accept and become comfortable with whatever label was being applied, while at the same time reminding himself of the complexity of his own true identity—an identity that can never be taken away, regardless of great success or awful failure.

It wasn't until 2017, fourteen years after Steve set the Texas state record in the mile, that he was able to fully move beyond the notion of being a failed running prodigy. In 2017, a runner named Sam Worley broke Steve's record. To Steve's surprise, he felt no sadness. And, perhaps even more surprising, outside of a few close family members and die-hard track fans, no one else even realized that he had lost the record. In that moment, it became crystal clear to Steve that, to a large extent, he had constructed his *own* identity as a failed runner and blown out of proportion the degree to which the outside world *actually* cared. To a small portion of the population that remembers his high school glory days, Steve may be known as a runner, or a 4:01-miler, or a prodigy-gone-bust. But for an entirely different population, he's known only as a coach or, for those reading this book, perhaps only as an author.

Our identities are constructs that result from what we reflect on others and what others reflect on us.

In other words, our identities are constructs that result

from what we reflect on others and what others reflect on us. The outside world is always stereotyping us, something over which we have little control. But as for our own sense of who we are—that, we do have a hand in. The story we tell ourselves about ourselves is who we become, and it's important to realize that until the day we die, this story is forever unfolding, constantly changing along with the ebb and flow of our lives. Though it can be a great challenge, nearly all of us can move beyond entrenched past identities to different future ones.

However, some people can't. And it's by examining these individuals that we learn even more about the massive importance of our internal narratives.

Passion Practices

- The way you craft your internal narrative, or the story you tell yourself about yourself, is critical to moving forward from a passion.
- When it's time to move forward from a passion, you shouldn't deny or suppress the fact that your passion was a big part of your life; rather, you should embrace that fact, and build upon the lessons learned and experiences gained from your past in whatever it is you do next.
- Rather than moving swiftly to the next thing, you should create some time and space to reflect upon your passion and the impact it had on your life.
- Although your activity or pursuit may change, the deep personality traits that fueled your passion don't. Harness these traits in the next chapter of your life.

. . .

AT SOME POINT OR ANOTHER, ALMOST EVERY CHILD AT-
tending school is faced with the same dilemma: remembering all
the facts and figures they've attempted to jam into their heads
over the last few months of study. If only they could remember
the date that the Allies stormed the beaches of Normandy, the
periodic table of elements, or what actually occurred in chapter 3 of *A Tale of Two Cities*. Mired in another late-night, last-
minute cramming session, teenagers around the world dream
of having a photographic memory, the ability to run accurate
Google searches in their minds. Some can.

A condition called hyperthymesia (also known as highly su-
perior autobiographical memory, or HSAM for short) is a form
of photographic memory. Individuals with HSAM have an un-
canny ability to recall past experiences with exacting detail.
Want to know, for example, what occurred in episode 3, season
6, of the TV show *Friends*? How about the score of a midsum-
mer Giants versus Astros baseball game in 1993? Or the names
of all the characters in Jonathan Franzen's novel *The Correc-
tions*? Someone with HSAM can recall these experiences with
precise accuracy, as long as they took part in the event in some
way (i.e., watched, read, listened to, or participated in it). In one
demonstration of this unique power, an individual with HSAM
lost a portion of her childhood diary. Decades later, she rewrote
all her childhood thoughts. The level of recall associated with
HSAM is utterly awesome.

The benefits of HSAM are readily apparent: Trivia contests
would be a breeze, a school system based on rote memorization
would be easily conquerable, and the ability to recall pretty
much anything with such exactitude—thus being able to no-

tice even the slightest changes over time—would surely come in handy in many professions. But what about the drawbacks?

Take for example, the common yet painful experience of getting over past relationships. The moment a breakup occurs, we begin to take control of the story we tell ourselves. The man or woman we had just a few days before gushed about—perhaps even telling friends and family how we might marry them—may suddenly shift to a despicable human being, or at the very least someone we're "better off without." We detail their shortcomings and tell ourselves all the reasons they were wrong for us and how, *in hindsight*, they treated us poorly. Over time, we may even try to delete them from our life: both figuratively (from our minds) and literally (from our Facebook feeds and photo albums). In other words, a large part of our moving on from a failed relationship is our ability to change our story.

On a recent episode of the radio show *This American Life*, Jill Price, an individual with HSAM, detailed a different experience of losing loved ones and breaking up with an ex.[9] She remembers every experience—the movies, the flowers, and the romantic dinners—as vividly as when they actually occurred. Even years after the fact, her recall is so detailed, so immersive, that she is essentially reliving each moment. Jill is left with a bitter reality: She cannot delude herself. There's no convincing herself that her ex was a bad guy, no overemphasizing the negative qualities and conveniently forgetting the good ones. Jill is left only with an unedited version of reality. She does not have the ability to change her story, to selectively frame her experience in a manner that allows her to move on.

Through individuals with HSAM, we get a glimpse of what happens when we lose control of our story, when we have no options for editing it and are stuck with only one interpretation of what occurred. Imagine a Hollywood producer who wants to bring the biography of a historical figure, like Abraham Lincoln, to life. Now imagine he's given two choices. In one, he's given a script that has to follow the exact details of the president's life. He's not allowed to shorten or cut any details that are not crucial to the main plot. If the producer follows through with such a script, he'll be left with a many-hours-long saga that drags on and will likely be a box office flop.

The second option is that he has creative license. He can smooth the rough edges while staying true to Lincoln's essence. He can fast-forward through the mundane parts of Lincoln's life to get to the points he wants to emphasize. He can downplay the portions of Lincoln's character that might have been a product of his time, and play up those that make him a hero to many. He can shorten Lincoln's life into a two-hour film with a plot that stays true to the man, but homes in on the main takeaways and cuts out many of the trivial details. In this second option, the producer has the capacity to craft the story in the way he needs to so that he can deliver a powerful message in a tightly wrapped production.

As you might have guessed, individuals who suffer from HSAM have only the first option—they literally can't forget or edit out certain details and emotions of past experiences. The rest of us, however, can edit our stories in a way that is conducive to our lives. In so many instances, we overcome hardships by making a director's cut, by smoothing out the rough edges of our past experiences.

THE ONLY THING THAT SHAPES YOUR IDENTITY MORE than the pursuit of your passions is your internal narrative: the story you tell yourself about yourself. How you write your story largely determines how you'll feel and what you'll do when you move on from a passion. This is empowering: If you can take control of and write your story, you can take control of and write your life. Much like Abby Wambach had the insight to realize, the magic is in the middle. Not just "the middle" as in during times of transition, the ever-important liminal spaces, but also in how you carry a past passion with you. While it's unhealthy for it to remain your entire identity, it's equally unhealthy to deny how it might have shaped you. Often, finding a middle ground is the best course.

IF YOU CAN TAKE CONTROL OF AND WRITE YOUR STORY, you can take control of and write your life.

Much like adopting the mastery mind-set and becoming more self-aware, writing your own story doesn't happen automatically. If anything, when moving on from a passion, the natural default is to succumb to negative emotions and try to fill the void with whatever is most readily available, which is why so many transition from productive passions to destructive addictions. Now that you're aware of this trap, you can take proactive steps to prevent it from happening. Pause and create the space you need to reflect on how you want to write your story. And whatever you write, ensure that it doesn't end with your passion, but rather builds upon it, taking the life experience gained from your passion and your deep personality traits that fueled it and embedding them into whatever comes next; moving not just onward but forward. It's human nature that your narrative will guide you. The direction it takes is up to you.

Living Productively with Passion

Commencement addresses and motivational speeches aren't likely to change anytime soon. Finding, following, and living with passion will remain common refrains. Whether this is a positive thing depends largely on who is receiving the message and how it is received. Mindlessly living with a passion can be extremely harmful and destructive. Mindfully living with a passion can be the key to a life well lived. Above all, *this* is the conclusion we came to after researching, reporting, and writing this book.

Mindfully living with a passion starts with realizing that passion in and of itself doesn't start off as either good or bad; it just *is*—a powerful emotion rooted in our biology and psychology. It's not something we magically find, but something that we develop by following our interests and incrementally devoting more of our time and energy to them. The next step to mindfully living with passion is to become aware of its dark side. Only by understanding the pitfalls of obsessive and fear-driven passion—and taking deliberate steps to avoid them—does passion gain the *potential* to be productive. But avoiding pitfalls is not enough. An equal challenge is bucking current trends that favor instant gratification and instead actively adopting the mastery mind-set: maintaining drive from within; focusing on the process over results; not worrying about being the best but worrying about being the best at getting better; embracing acute failure for chronic gains; practicing patience; and paying full attention to our pursuits. Cultivating these practices opens the door

Mindlessly living with a passion can be extremely harmful and destructive. Mindfully living with a passion can be the key to a life well lived.

to harmonious passion, the best kind of passion, and the special kind of Quality it manifests. Even so, it is important to remember that harmony with a passion can still lead to disharmony in other areas of your life. "Balance" is more often than not an illusion, *especially* for someone who is wholly absorbed in a passion.

Instead of striving for balance, then, the passionate person should strive to be self-aware. Self-awareness—which, paradoxically, comes from distancing yourself from your "self"—is the only force strong enough to counter passion's overwhelming inertia. Self-awareness ensures that you control your passion rather than your passion controlling you. It allows you to honestly evaluate what your passion is costing you, and to *choose* how to go forward as a result. So long as your passion is harmonious and you are aware of what you're sacrificing to pursue it, then there is no "wrong" choice. The only wrong choice is losing the ability to consciously make one. Whatever choice you make about how to pursue your passion, about how much of your time and energy it should consume, it's critical that you do so as the author of your own story. Although your passion can be an integral part of that story, it should never be the entire thing. It is imperative that you write chapters that build upon and branch out from your passion—your life may very well depend on it.

Unfortunately, these are the lessons that the commencement and motivational speakers don't mention. They may not fit into nice sound bites, and they certainly aren't all positive. Yet they are the true keys to finding and living with passion, even if the truth is hard, uncomfortable, and messy.

In the final analysis, passion can turn into an incredible, life-giving energy, but it can also turn into a destructive, life-sapping storm. Passion moves the world forward. It fills people with life and joy, yet it can also end in sadness and depression. It leads to Olympic medals, and it leads to Olympic cheaters. It births marriages, and it destroys marriages. It can lead to immense creativity or debilitating addiction. Passion is perhaps the most overwhelming emotion there is.

Whether it's a gift or a curse—that's largely up to you.

Acknowledgments

Writing this book was another team effort—not only between the two of us, but also between us and so many other individuals who contributed in their own unique ways. If you enjoyed *The Passion Paradox*, please join us in a moment of thanks for the following people:

First and foremost, we want to thank our core team, who continue to support our work and take it to the next level. To Caitlin Stulberg, who once again showed that she is not just an unbelievable wife to one of us, but also an unbelievable editor to both of us. Nearly every page of this book—and one of its authors—is better because of her.

To our agent, Ted Weinstein, who continues to push our thinking and who is never shy about telling us what he thinks—which is exactly what you want in an agent.

To our acquiring editor, Mark Weinstein, who began encouraging us to write this book less than a week after he published our first one. He believed in the concept from the get-go, and he also believed in us.

And to our current editor, Donna Loffredo. Shortly after we had completed our first draft of the manuscript, our old publisher was sold to the Crown Publishing Group at Penguin Random House. To be completely honest, we had no clue what would happen or what to expect. Well, what happened was this: Donna made the book her own and she exceeded all of our expectations. She took our initial draft and pushed the concept (and the writing) even further. The result is a richer, more elegant, and more insightful book. Donna, you've become the perfect partner. We're so fortunate that the universe put this book and us as authors into your hands. In addition to Donna, we'd also like to thank the whole team at Crown. Brianne Sperber, Connie Capone, and Shauna Barry led a strong charge to ensure this book would reach as many readers as possible. Ivy McFadden and Alisa Garrison caught all our grammatical errors and made the copy shine.

We also want to thank the readers of our early drafts; your feedback improved this book immensely. Thank you to Zack Bloom, Emily Magness, Hillary Montgomery, Alan McClain, Andy Stover, and Brian Barraza.

And we'd like to thank our mentors and close friends, who encouraged us to write this book and whose collective impression on us over the years shaped its message. We are fortunate to have lifelong teachers, and we are blessed to be surrounded by a circle of wisdom, kindness, and caring. A special thanks to Justin Bosley, David Epstein, Mario Fraioli, Vern Gambetta, Adam Grant, Bruce Grierson, Michaela Hoffman, Alex Hutchinson, Jon Marcus, Danny Mackey, Mike Joyner, Bob Kocher, Kelly McGonigal, Rich Roll, and Melissa Stern.

Thanks are also in order to the publications to which we regularly contribute, including *Outside* magazine (in particular, Brad's editors Wesley Judd and Matt Skenazy) and *New York* magazine (in particular, Brad's editor Melissa Dahl). Some of the stories and insights in this book first appeared in Brad's columns in both *Outside* and *New York*. It's truly an honor to write regularly for such first-rate publications.

And of course, thanks to all the passionate people whose stories we shared in this book and who have helped us come to realize everything that we wrote. While there are far too many to name, we want to call out all of Steve's athletes and Brad's coaching clients, whom we are privileged to work with on this stuff every day.

Finally, thanks to the members of our families, who have always supported us in pursuing our own passions. Without them, none of this would be possible. Caitlin Stulberg, Linda and Bob Stulberg, Eric Stulberg, Lois Stulberg, Bob and Elaine Appel, Randee and Bob Bloom, William and Elizabeth Magness, Phillip and Emily Magness: Thank you.

Notes

1: PASSION MUST BE HANDLED WITH CARE

1. C. Jordan, "Gown Alert: Bon Jovi to Address Rutgers-Camden Commencement," *app.*, April 3, 2015, http://www.app.com/story /entertainment/2015/04/03/gown-alert-bon-jovi-to-address -rutgers-camden-commencement/70873794/.
2. Elon Musk (@elonmusk), "The reality is great highs, terrible lows, and unrelenting stress. Don't think people want to hear about the last two," Twitter, July 30, 2017, 1:23 p.m., https://twitter.com /elonmusk/status/891710778205626368.

2: THE ORIGINS OF PASSION: A BRIEF HISTORY OF SUFFERING AND LOVE

1. Interview with Timothy K. Beal, August 12, 2016.
2. W. Shakespeare, *Titus Andronicus*, Act II, Scene I, http://shake speare.mit.edu/titus/full.html.
3. A. Dreber et al., "The 7R Polymorphism in the Dopamine Receptor D4 Gene (DRD4) Is Associated with Financial Risk Taking in Men," *Evolution and Human Behavior* 30, no. 2 (March 2009): 85–92, http://www.sciencedirect.com/science/article/pii/S1090513 808001165.
4. Interview with Ann Trason, conducted by Brad for his article "What's Behind the Relentless Pursuit of Excellence?," *Outside*, March 7, 2016.
5. D. H. Zald et al., "Midbrain Dopamine Receptor Availability Is Inversely Associated with Novelty-Seeking Traits in Humans," *Journal of Neuroscience* 28, no. 53 (December 31, 2008): 14377, http://www.jneurosci.org/content/28/53/14372.short.

6. M. Lewis, PhD, *The Biology of Desire: Why Addiction Is Not a Disease* (New York: PublicAffairs, 2016), 42.

7. "The 2009 MF 25," *Men's Journal*, https://www.mensjournal.com/health-fitness/2009-mf-25.

8. Series of author interviews with Rich Roll, August 2016.

9. Interview with Alan St Clair Gibson, conducted by Brad for "What's Behind the Relentless Pursuit of Excellence?"

10. D. Collins and A. MacNamara, "The Rocky Road to the Top: Why Talent Needs Trauma," *Sports Medicine* 42, no. 11 (September 2012): 907–14, https://www.ncbi.nlm.nih.gov/pubmed/23013519.

11. Interview with Gibson for "What's Behind the Relentless Pursuit of Excellence?"

12. M. Lewis, *The New New Thing: A Silicon Valley Story* (New York: W. W. Norton, 2014), 58.

13. Ibid.

14. Lewis, *Biology of Desire*, 66.

15. M. Szalavitz, "The 4 Traits That Put Kids at Risk for Addiction," *New York Times*, September 29, 2016.

16. P. Conrod et al., "Effectiveness of a Selective, Personality-Targeted Prevention Program for Adolescent Alcohol Use and Misuse: A Cluster Randomized Controlled Trial," *JAMA Psychiatry* 70, no. 3 (March 2013): 334–42, https://www.ncbi.nlm.nih.gov/pubmed/23344135.

17. M. Szalavitz, *Unbroken Brain: A Revolutionary New Way of Understanding Addiction* (New York: Picador, 2017), 7.

3: FIND AND GROW YOUR PASSION

1. Marist Poll "Do you believe in the idea of soul mates, that is, two people who are destined to be together?," January 6–10, 2011, http://maristpoll.marist.edu/wp-content/misc/usapolls/US110106/Soul%20Mates/Americans_Who_Believe_in_Soul_Mates.htm.

2. C. R. Knee, H. Patrick, N. Vietor, and C. Neighbors, "Implicit Theories of Relationships: Moderators of the Link Between Conflict and Commitment," *Personality and Social Psychology Bulletin* 30, no. 5 (May 2004): 617–28.

3. P. Chen, P. C. Ellsworth, and N. Schwarz, "Finding a Fit or Developing It: Implicit Theories About Achieving Passion for Work,"

Personality and Social Psychology Bulletin 41, no. 10 (October 2015): 1411–24, DOI: 10.1177/0146167215596988.

4. Chen et al., "Finding a Fit or Developing It."

5. G. Pezzulo and P. Cisek, "Navigating the Affordance Landscape: Feedback Control as a Process Model of Behavior and Cognition," *Trends in Cognitive Sciences* 20, no. 6 (June 2016): 414–24, https://doi.org/10.1016/j.tics.2016.03.013.

6. R. Ryan and E. Deci, "Self-Determination Theory and the Facilitation of Intrinsic Motivation, Social Development, and Well-Being," *American Psychologist* 55, no. 1 (January 2000): 68–78, DOI: 10.1037110003-066X.55.1.68.

7. D. Liu, X. P. Chen, and X. Yao, "From Autonomy to Creativity: A Multilevel Investigation of the Mediating Role of Harmonious Passion," *Journal of Applied Psychology* 96, no. 2 (March 2011): 294–309, DOI: 10.1037/a0021294.

8. E. Luna, *The Crossroads of Should and Must* (New York: Workman, 2015), 25.

9. J. Raffiee and J. Feng, "Should I Quit My Day Job?: A Hybrid Path to Entrepreneurship," *Academy of Management Journal* 57, no. 4 (October 2013): 948, https://doi.org/10.5465/amj.2012.0522.

10. *Harvard Business Review,* "Why Going All-In on Your Start-Up Might Not Be the Best Idea," August 2014, https://hbr.org/2014/08/why-going-all-in-on-your-start-up-might-not-be-the-best-idea.

11. M. Lewis, *Moneyball* (New York: W. W. Norton & Company, 2003), 193.

12. N. N. Taleb, *Antifragile* (New York: Random House, 2014), 161–7.

13. B. Stulberg, "No One Wants to Talk About Death, but You Need to Anyway," *Los Angeles Times,* December 30, 2013.

14. Luna, *Crossroads of Should and Must,* 34.

15. Thich Nhat Hanh, *The Heart of the Buddha's Teaching* (New York: Broadway Books, 1999), 185.

4: WHEN PASSION GOES AWRY

1. P. Lattman, "Enron: Skilling and Petrocelli's Passion Play," *Wall Street Journal Law Blog* (blog), May 16, 2006.

2. N. Stein, "The World's Most Admired Companies," *Fortune,* October 2, 2000.

3. M. McFarland, "'This Is What I Was Put on Earth to Do': Elizabeth Holmes and the Importance of Passion," *Washington Post,* October 12, 2015.

4. McFarland, "'This Is What I Was Put on Earth to Do.'"
5. N. Bilton, "Exclusive: How Elizabeth Holmes's House of Cards Came Tumbling Down," *Vanity Fair*, September 2016.
6. HHS filing against Elizabeth Holmes, http://online.wsj.com/public/resources/documents/cms20160412.pdf.
7. S. Buhr, "Theranos Reaches Settlement with Investor Partner Fund Management," TechCrunch, May 1, 2017.
8. S. A. O'Brien, "Theranos Founder Elizabeth Holmes Charged with Massive Fraud," *CNNMoney* (blog), CNN, March 14, 2018.
9. Epictetus, *Discourses and Selected Writings*, ed. R. Dobbin (New York: Penguin Classics, 2008), 175.
10. E. Fromm, *To Have or to Be?* (New York: Harper & Row, 1976), 63.
11. D. Whyte, *The Three Marriages: Reimagining Work, Self and Relationship* (New York: Riverhead Books, 2010), 155.
12. A. Wilson and L. Potwarka, "Exploring Relationships Between Passion and Attitudes Toward Performance-Enhancing Drugs in Canadian Collegiate Sports Contexts," *Journal of Intercollegiate Sport* 8, no. 2 (December 2015): 227–46, https://doi.org/10.1123/jis.2014-0093.
13. World Anti-Doping Agency, "Death for Performance—What would athletes trade-off for success?," https://www.wada-ama.org/sites/default/files/resources/files/connor_project_summary.pdf.
14. D. Schawbel, "Alex Rodriguez: What Most People Don't Know About Being a Top Athlete," *Forbes*, May 18, 2016.
15. D. Moceanu, *Off Balance: A Memoir* (New York: Touchstone, 2013), 115.
16. Ibid., 141.
17. J. J. Bélanger, M.-A. K. Lafrenière, R. J. Vallerand, and A. W. Kruglanski, "Driven by Fear: The Effect of Success and Failure Information on Passionate Individuals' Performance," *Journal of Personality and Social Psychology* 104, no. 1 (2013): 180–95, http://dx.doi.org/10.1037/a0029585.
18. K. Starr, "The Downside of Following Passion," *The Atlantic*, September 5, 2012.
19. D. E. Conroy, J. P. Willow, and J. N. Metzler, "Multidimensional Fear of Failure Measurement: The Performance Failure Appraisal Inventory," *Journal of Applied Sport Psychology* 14, no. 2 (2002): 76–90, DOI: 10.1080/10413200252907752.
20. S. Beecham, *Elite Minds: How Winners Think Differently to Create*

a Competitive Edge and Maximize Success (New York: McGraw-Hill Education, 2016), 67.

5: THE BEST KIND OF PASSION

1. Fromm, *To Have or to Be?*, 51.
2. C. Gaines, "Katie Ledecky Explains Why She Is Passing Up an Estimated $5 Million per Year in Endorsements," *Business Insider*, August 24, 2016.
3. E. B. Falk, M. B. O'Donnell, C. N. Cascio, et al., "Self-Affirmation Alters the Brain's Response to Health Messages and Subsequent Behavior Change," *PNAS* 112, no. 7 (February 2015): 1977–82; published ahead of print February 2, 2015, https://doi.org/10.1073/pnas.1500247112.
4. R. M. Rilke, *Letters to a Young Poet* (Novato, CA: New World Library), 16.
5. W. T. Gallwey, *The Inner Game of Tennis: The Classic Guide to the Mental Side of Peak Performance* (New York: Random House, 1997), 116–7.
6. B. Stulberg, "Big Goals Can Backfire. Olympians Show Us What to Focus on Instead," *New York*, August 3, 2016.
7. M. W. Howe, P. L. Tierney, S. G. Sandberg, et al., "Prolonged Dopamine Signalling in Striatum Signals Proximity and Value of Distant Rewards," *Nature* 500, no. 7464 (August 2013): 575–9, DOI: 10.1038/nature12475.
8. Y. Goto and A. A. Grace, "Dopaminergic Modulation of Limbic and Cortical Drive of Nucleus Accumbens in Goal-Directed Behavior," *Nature Neuroscience* 8, no. 5 (May 2005): 805–12, https://doi.org/10.1038/nn1471.
9. D. Collins, A. MacNamara, and N. McCarthy, "Super Champions, Champions, and Almosts: Important Differences and Commonalities on the Rocky Road," *Frontiers in Psychology* 6, no. 2009 (January 2016): 1–11, DOI: 10.3389/fpsyg.2015.02009.
10. Amazon SEC filing, http://phx.corporate-ir.net/phoenix.zhtml?c=97664&p=irol-SECText&TEXT=aHR0cDovL2FwaS50ZW5r d2l6YXJkLmNvbS9maWxpbmcueG1sP2lwYWdlPTk1MjIwMzg mRFNFUT0wJlNFUT0wJlNRREVTQz1TRUNUSU9OX0VOVOV ElSRSZzdWJzaWQ9NTc%3d.
11. J. S. Moser, H. S. Schroder, C. Heeter, et al., "Mind Your Errors: Evidence for a Neural Mechanism Linking Growth Mind-Set to

Adaptive Posterror Adjustments," *Psychological Science* 22, no. 12 (October 2011): 1484–9, DOI: 10.1177/0956797611419520.

12. T. D. Wilson, D. A. Reinhard, E. C. Westgate, et al., "Just Think: The Challenges of the Disengaged Mind," *Science* 345, no. 6192 (July 2014): 75–7, https://doi.org/10.1126/science.1250830.

13. G. Leonard, *The Way of Aikido: Life Lessons from an American Sensei* (New York: Plume, 2000), 171 (emphasis added).

14. G. Leonard, *Mastery: The Keys to Success and Long-Term Fulfillment* (New York: Plume, 1992), 21–3.

15. G. Leonard, ed., "Playing for Keeps: The Art of Mastery in Sport and Life," *Esquire*, May 1987.

16. R. M. Pirsig, *Zen and the Art of Motorcycle Maintenance* (New York: HarperTorch, 2006), 171.

17. M. Crawford, *Shop Class as Soulcraft* (New York: Penguin Press, 2009), 194.

18. A. de Botton, *How Proust Can Change Your Life* (New York: Pantheon, 1997).

19. R. Friedman, A. Fishbach, J. Förster, and L. Werth, "Attentional Priming Effects on Creativity," *Creativity Research Journal* 15, nos. 2–3 (2003): 277–86, https://doi.org/10.1080/10400419.2003.9651420.

20. A. Dijksterhuis and H. Aarts, "Goals, Attention, and (Un)consciousness," *Annual Review of Psychology* 61 (January 2010): 467–90, DOI: 10.1146/annurev.psych.093008.100445.

21. Pirsig, *Zen and the Art of Motorcycle Maintenance*, 299–310.

22. Leonard, *Mastery*, 40.

23. Fromm, *To Have or to Be?*, 117–8.

24. F. Mullan, "A Founder of Quality Assessment Encounters a Troubled System Firsthand," *Health Affairs* 20, no. 1 (January/February 2001): 137–41, https://doi.org/10.1377/hlthaff.20.1.137.

25. T. Curran, A. P. Hill, P. R. Appleton, et al., "The Psychology of Passion: A Meta-Analytical Review of a Decade of Research on Intrapersonal Outcomes," *Motivation and Emotion* 39, no. 5 (2015): 631–55, http://dx.doi.org/10.1007/s11031-015-9503-0.

6: THE ILLUSION OF BALANCE

1. E. J. Rohn, *Leading an Inspired Life* (Chicago: Nightingale Conant, 2010).

2. George Washington University, "Demand Work-Life Balance Training," https://hr.gwu.edu.

3. B. Stulberg, "Maybe We All Need a Little Less Balance," *Well* (blog), *New York Times*, August 22, 2017.

4. L. Du, "Warren Buffett's High School Yearbook Foreshadowed His Future Career," *Business Insider*, June 6, 2012.

5. J. Surowiecki, "'Becoming Warren Buffett,' The Man, Not the Investor," *New Yorker*, January 31, 2017.

6. *Becoming Warren Buffett*, directed by Peter Kunhardt; HBO Documentary Films, January 30, 2017.

7. Surowiecki, "'Becoming Warren Buffett,' The Man, Not the Investor."

8. S. Begum, "The Son Gandhi Disowned," *Manchester Evening News*, August 20, 2007.

9. Aristotle, *The Nicomachean Ethics*, ed. Lesley Brown, trans. David Ross (Oxford, UK: Oxford University Press, 2005), 190 (emphasis added).

10. B. Stulberg, "Shalane Flanagan on How to Achieve Peak Performance," *Outside*, February 21, 2018.

11. D. S. Ridley, P. A. Schutz, R. S. Glanz, and C. E. Weinstein, "Self-Regulated Learning: The Interactive Influence of Metacognitive Awareness and Goal-Setting," *Journal of Experimental Education* 60, no. 4 (1992): 293–306, http://dx.doi.org/10.1080/00220973.1992.9943867; S. L. Franzoi, M. H. Davis, and R. D. Young, "The Effects of Private Self-Consciousness and Perspective Taking on Satisfaction in Close Relationships," *Journal of Personality and Social Psychology* 48, no. 6 (June 1985): 1584–94; P. J. Silvia and M. E. O'Brien, "Self-Awareness and Constructive Functioning: Revisiting the Human Dilemma," *Journal of Social and Clinical Psychology* 23, no. 4 (August 2004): 475–89, DOI: 10.1521/jscp.23.4.475.40307.

12. C. R. Cloninger, "The Science of Well-Being: An Integrated Approach to Mental Health and Its Disorders," *World Psychiatry* 5, no. 2 (June 2006): 71–6.

7: SELF-AWARENESS AND THE POWER TO CHOOSE

1. S. Lindley, *Surfacing: From the Depths of Self-Doubt to Winning Big and Living Fearlessly* (Boulder, CO: VeloPress, 2016), 183.

2. R. Ellison, *The Invisible Man* (New York: Vintage, 1995), 103.

3. S. Vazire and E. N. Carlson, "Others Sometimes Know Us Better Than We Know Ourselves," *Current Directions in Psychological Science* 20, no. 2 (2011): 104–8, DOI: 10.1177/0963721411402478.

4. K. Crouse, "Adam Rippon on Quiet Starvation in Men's Figure Skating," *New York Times*, February 2, 2018.

5. B. Stulberg, "To Navigate a Challenge, Pretend You're Giving Advice to a Friend," *The Cut* (blog), *New York*, February 21, 2017.

6. I. Grossmann and E. Kross, "Exploring Solomon's Paradox: Self-Distancing Eliminates the Self-Other Asymmetry in Wise Reasoning About Close Relationships in Younger and Older Adults," *Psychological Science* 25, no. 8 (August 2014): 1571–80, https://doi.org/10.1177%2F0956797614535400.

7. A. Rivas, "Writing in the Third Person Helps Stressed People Understand Their Circumstances More Wisely," *Medical Daily*, June 10, 2014, http://www.medicaldaily.com/writing-third-person-helps-stressed-people-understand-their-circumstances-more-wisely-287460.

8. Ö. Ayduk and E. Kross, "From a Distance: Implications of Spontaneous Self-Distancing for Adaptive Self-Reflection," *Journal of Personality and Social Psychology* 98, no. 5 (May 2010): 809–29, DOI: 10.1037/a0019205.

9. R. Garan, "Seeing Earth from Space," *Fragile Oasis* (blog), September 26, 2013, http://www.fragileoasis.org/blog/2013/9/seeing-earth-from-space/.

10. F. White, *The Overview Effect: Space Exploration and Human Evolution* (Reston, VA: American Institute of Aeronautics and Astronautics, 1998), 1.

11. D. Keltner, "Why Do We Feel Awe?," *Greater Good*, May 10, 2016, http://greatergood.berkeley.edu/article/item/why_do_we_feel_awe.

12. D. Keltner and J. Haidt, "Approaching Awe, a Moral, Spiritual, and Aesthetic Emotion," *Cognition and Emotion* 17, no. 2 (2003): 297–314, https://doi.org/10.1080/02699930302297.

13. K. Tippett, *Becoming Wise: An Inquiry into the Mystery and Art of Living* (New York: Penguin Books, 2017), 12.

14. D. Keltner, "Why Do We Feel Awe?"

15. Seneca, *Moral Letters to Lucilius*, vol. 3, trans. R. M. Gummere (Toronto, ON: Aegitas Digital Publishing, 2015), loc. 106, ebook.

16. J. Kabat-Zinn, *Wherever You Go, There You Are: Mindfulness Meditation in Everyday Life* (New York: Hachette Books, 2005), xvi.

17. Seneca, *On the Shortness of Life: Life Is Long If You Know How to Use It*, trans. C. D. N. Costa (New York: Penguin Books, 2005), 13.

18. N. Riggs, *The Bright Hour: A Memoir of Living and Dying* (New York: Simon & Schuster, 2017), 243.

8: MOVING ON: HOW TO TRANSITION FROM A PASSION WITH GRACE AND GRIT

1. A. Wambach, *Forward: A Memoir* (New York: Dey Street Books, 2016), 32.
2. Ibid., 161–70.
3. M. S. Gazzaniga, "The Split Brain in Man," *Scientific American* 217, no. 2 (1967): 24–9, http://dx.doi.org/10.1038/scientific american0867-24.
4. C. S. Dweck, *Mindset: The New Psychology of Success* (New York: Ballantine Books, 2007).
5. M. Kees, L. S. Nerenberb, J. Bachrach, and L. A. Sommer, "Changing the Personal Narrative: A Pilot Study of a Resiliency Intervention for Military Spouses," *Contemporary Family Therapy* 37, no. 3 (September 2015): 221–31, https://doi.org/10.1007/s10591 -015-9336-8.
6. Tippett, *Becoming Wise*, 52.
7. Wambach, *Forward*, 171–2.
8. Ibid., 228.
9. *This American Life*, episode 585, "In Defense of Ignorance," NPR, April 22, 2016, https://www.thisamericanlife.org/radio -archives/episode/585/in-defense-of-ignorance.

Index

About the Authors

Brad Stulberg coaches, researches, writes, and speaks on health and human performance. His coaching practice includes working with athletes, entrepreneurs, and executives on their performance and well-being. He is a columnist at *Outside* and has written for the *New York Times*, *New York* magazine, *Sports Illustrated*, *Wired*, *Forbes*, and the *Los Angeles Times*. Previously, Stulberg worked as a consultant for McKinsey & Company, where he counseled some of the world's top executives on a broad range of issues. An avid athlete and outdoor enthusiast, Stulberg lives in Oakland, California, with his wife, son, and two cats. Follow him on Twitter @BStulberg.

Steve Magness coaches some of the top distance runners in the world and has propelled numerous athletes to Olympic trials, world championship teams, and the Olympics. Known widely for his integration of science and practice, Steve has been on the forefront of innovation in sport. He has been a featured expert in *Runner's World*, the *New York Times*, the *New Yorker*, BBC, the *Wall Street Journal*, and *ESPN The Magazine*. His first book, *The Science of Running*, was published in 2014. He lives in Houston, Texas. Follow him on Twitter @SteveMagness.

ALSO BY
BRAD STULBERG AND
STEVE MAGNESS

RODALE.

AVAILABLE WHEREVER BOOKS ARE SOLD.